AREOPAGITICA
and
OF EDUCATION

# Crofts Classics

## GENERAL EDITORS

Samuel H. Beer, *Harvard University*

O. B. Hardison, Jr., *The Folger Shakespeare Library*

Eric Bentley

On the cover is reproduced an etching of Westminster Hall, by Wenceslas Hollar (1607–77). Hollar was born in Prague, studied in Frankfurt, and worked in Strasbourg and Cologne until 1636 when his topographical scenes attacted the attention of the Earl of Arundel, who was traveling on an embassy to Vienna. Lord Arundel took him back to England with him. Unlike Milton, Hollar supported the King in his unsuccessful struggle against Parliament and decided to escape to Antwerp in 1644, returning in 1652. Westminster Hall was built in 1097 by William II and enlarged by his successors, reaching its present form in 1399. From the fifteenth century till 1882 it was the seat of the chief law courts, and it was here that Charles I was condemned in 1649. Reproduced by permission of the New York Public Library, Prints Division, Astor, Lenox and Tilden Foundations.

*Research for cover art by Nigel Foxell.*

# JOHN MILTON

# Areopagitica

AND

# Of Education

With Autobiographical Passages
from Other Prose Works

EDITED BY

*George H. Sabine*
CORNELL UNIVERSITY

AHM Publishing Corporation
Northbrook, Illinois 60062

ISBN: 0-88295-057-6
(Formerly 0-390-22980-6)

Library of Congress Card Number: 51-6754

PRINTED IN THE UNITED STATES OF AMERICA
7115
FOURTEENTH PRINTING

# CONTENTS

# INTRODUCTION

THE TWO SMALL works here reprinted make up that portion of Milton's prose which has been most continuously read and which has been held in ever higher esteem with the passage of time. Together they express more fully than any other of his prose writings the characteristic bent of his genius, which has been called Christian humanism. Both were inspired by the thought which dominated the middle period of his life, the hope that the Puritan Revolution would prove to be a national regeneration alike in religion and in politics. The tractate *Of Education* offered Milton's plan for training a ruling class in a society thus regenerated, a class at once intellectually and artistically cultivated, morally elevated and devoted, and civic-minded. The end of education it defined as equally "to know God aright" and to fit men "to perform justly, skilfully, and magnanimously" all the duties of public and private life; the essence of Milton's thought lay in the presumption that these purposes are identical. Hence education must be comprehensive, addressed to the physical, intellectual, aesthetic, moral, and religious faculties. Conducted exclusively through the ancient languages, its linguistic side was still instrumental, to give access to the "solid things" contained therein. In this respect it embodied the best ideal of a classical and liberal education. Yet here also lay its weakness as the model for a modern education. Milton belonged to the last generation that could reasonably regard ancient knowledge as containing all that an educated man needs to know—of natural science, of statecraft, as well as of literature. The Reformation and the Renaissance, by which his mind was formed, consciously looked toward the past. They envisaged a modern society as recovering the purity of primitive Christianity or the wisdom of the ancient sage. Yet the decade that produced Milton's two pamphlets saw also the first meetings of those scholars, dedicated to the pursuit of "experimental philosophy," who organized the Royal Society "to improve the knowledge of natural things." For better or worse natural science, with its implication of never ending change, turned modern society unescapably toward the future. For education it created the problem of uniting change with stability.

The writing of the *Areopagitica* had a personal occasion. This was a lively controversy that arose in 1644 over religious toleration. The Westminster Assembly of Divines, appointed to advise Parliament on religious reform, was prevailingly Presbyterian but contained a few Independents or Congregationalists. These latter published a defense of toleration (entitled *An Apologetical Narration*), and the Presbyterian majority incited Parliament to enforce the licensing law against the authors, and also against Roger Williams and Milton. In August a sermon was preached before Parliament in which one of Milton's pamphlets on divorce was attacked as "a wicked book." About the same time the Stationers' Company petitioned for a stricter enforcement of the licensing law and named Milton as a violator, which in fact he was, since some of his pamphlets had been issued without license. The *Areopagitica* was Milton's reply.

The practice of censorship had long been in effect when Milton wrote. It had been exercised, as he said, not in accord with any "ancient statute" but by royal decree and especially through the Court of Star Chamber. Milton might well argue, therefore, that it should share the odium attaching to that organ of personal government. When Star Chamber was abolished in 1641 control of the press passed to Parliament, which enacted in 1643 the law against which the *Areopagitica* was directed. This law really continued in force a decree of Star Chamber issued in 1637, with one change in administration. Whereas licensing had been exercised principally by the Archbishop of Canterbury and the Bishop of London, under the new law a Committee of

Examinations was appointed. These were the "twenty licensers" frequently mentioned in the *Areopagitica*. At the time when Milton began to publish, however, between the opening of the Long Parliament and the law of 1643, the press had been practically free. Hence Milton might reasonably hope that this freedom was part of a general policy of liberation. In truth the Presbyterian party in Parliament had no more intention of adopting such a policy than the party of Archbishop Laud which they replaced. The *Areopagitica* could make no headway against the violent partisanship of its time. Not until 1694 did licensing disappear from English legislation.

Yet in time the *Areopagitica* became the classic literary defense in English of intellectual liberty and freedom of publication. With Locke's *Letters on Toleration* and Mill's essay *On Liberty* it expressed the profoundest moral conviction that has underlaid the political thought of the English speaking peoples, but in eloquence and passion the *Areopagitica* far surpassed the other two. Its basic principle was the right and also the duty of every intelligent man, as a rational being, to know the grounds and to take the responsibility for his beliefs and his actions. Its corollary was a society and a state in which decisions are reached by open discussion, in which the sources of information are not contaminated by authority in the interest of party, and in which political unity is secured not by force but by a consensus that respects variety of opinion. These beliefs are permanent and indispensable elements of individual liberty and a free society; they do not depend upon the particular points of doctrine, theological or political, that concerned Milton and sometimes limited his view.

The *Areopagitica* did not in fact fully accept the principles of freedom which its argument assumed. Milton's Protestantism was never able to concede religious toleration to Roman Catholics. Neither was his belief in freedom expressly democratic, though it was perhaps so by implication. He said that censorship in effect "held the people for an untaught and irreligious, gadding rout," but he himself described them as "a herd confused, a miscellaneous rabble." By temperament and by conviction Milton was an intellectual aristocrat; the freedom which he meant to defend was primarily for scholars, not for "children and childish men." His political ideals were derived from the ancient aristocratic republic in which "the best and wisest men," not the generality of men, were supposed to rule. Yet in principle Milton's argument for complete freedom of writing and reading is untenable unless one assumes that all men in their degree are capable of reason and moral responsibility.

Milton's thought combined the essential ideas of the Protestant Reformation and the Renaissance. From the former he distilled the ideal of a religion without ritual or priestcraft but with its moral imperatives powerfully re-enforced, in which the individual Christian, having no mediator between himself and God except conscience, finds in his own personally formed convictions a supreme and a sufficient guide of conduct. From the latter he derived an ideal of personal distinction and intellectual independence cultivated by the study of Greek literature and philosophy and strengthened by the Roman sense of duty and civic obligation. Like Puritanism in general, Milton's Christianity was formed rather upon the prophetic books of the Old Testament than upon the New; it was a religion less of love than of duty and devotion. Between these three—the passion of the Hebrew prophet, the Protestant sense of the immediacy of God, and the free intelligence of classical antiquity—Milton saw no incompatibility. His humanism was an effort to fuse them into the single ideal of a complete personality, marked by broad learning, fastidious taste, and an intense personal and political idealism. His apostrophe to England at the end of the *Areopagitica* was his vision of this ideal realized in the Puritan Revolution, which he hoped might be "the reforming of reformation itself."

# PRINCIPAL DATES IN THE LIFE OF JOHN MILTON

1608    Born, London, December 9.

1625    Entered Christ's College, Cambridge.

1629    Bachelor of Arts.

1632    Master of Arts.

1632–38 Continued his studies in his father's house at Horton, Buckinghamshire. Wrote "Comus," "Lycidas"; possibly "L'Allegro," "Il Penseroso."

1638–39 Travelled in Italy. Settled in London and taught private pupils until 1647.

1640    Opening of the Long Parliament.

1641–42 Five pamphlets against prelacy, or the episcopal form of church government. The Bishops excluded from Parliament, 1641. First marriage, to Mary Powell, 1642.

1040    Westminster Assembly appointed to settle the form of church government. Parliament renews the order forbidding unlicensed printing.

1644–45 Four pamphlets on divorce.

1644    *Of Education, Areopagitica.*

1645    King Charles's army defeated at Naseby.

1646    Published collected poems.

1649    Execution of Charles I. Two political tracts. Appointed Secretary for Foreign Tongues to the Council of State.

1651    *Pro populo Anglicano defensio* (Defense of the People of England).

1652    Becomes totally blind. Death of Mary Milton.

1653    Cromwell becomes Lord Protector.

1654    *Pro populo Anglicano defensio secunda* (Second Defense).

1656    Second marriage, to Katherine Woodcock.

1658    Death of Katherine Milton. Death of Cromwell.

1659    Two pamphlets on separation of church and state.

1660    Pamphlet on a Free Commonwealth. Restoration of the monarchy. Milton imprisoned for a short time.

1663    Third marriage, to Elizabeth Minshull.

1667    *Paradise Lost.*

1671    *Paradise Regained, Samson Agonistes.*

1674    Died, November 8.

# AREOPAGITICA[1]

## A SPEECH FOR THE LIBERTY OF UNLICENSED
## PRINTING, TO THE PARLIAMENT OF ENGLAND

> This is true liberty, when free-born men,
> Having to advise the public, may speak free,
> Which he who can, and will, deserves high praise;
> Who neither can nor will, may hold his peace;
> What can be juster in a State than this?
>
> EURIPIDES, *The Suppliants*

THEY WHO to states[2] and governors of the commonwealth direct their speech, High Court of Parliament, or wanting[3] such access in a private condition, write that which they foresee may advance the public good; I suppose them, as at the beginning of no mean endeavor, not a little altered[4] and moved inwardly in their minds: some with doubt of what will be the success,[5] others with fear of what will be the censure;[6] some with hope, others with confidence of what they have to speak. And me perhaps each of these dispositions, as the subject was whereon I entered, may have at other times variously affected; and likely might in these foremost expressions now also disclose which of them swayed most, but that the very attempt of this address thus made, and the thought of whom it hath recourse to, hath got the power within me to a passion far more welcome than incidental to a preface.[7]

[1] Areopagitica Milton adopted his title from the Areopagitic Oration of Isocrates, written in 355 B.C. [2] states rulers [3] wanting lacking [4] altered perturbed [5] success result [6] censure opinion [7] power . . . preface raised me to a height of feeling more welcome than likely to occur in a preface

1

Which though I stay not to confess ere any ask, I shall be blameless, if it be no other than the joy and gratulation which it brings to all who wish and promote their country's liberty;[8] whereof this whole discourse proposed will be a certain testimony, if not a trophy.[9] For this is not the liberty which we can hope, that no grievance ever should arise in the commonwealth: that let no man in this world expect; but when complaints are freely heard, deeply considered, and speedily reformed, then is the utmost bound of civil liberty attained that wise men look for. To which if I now manifest, by the very sound of this which I shall utter, that we are already in good part arrived, and yet from such a steep disadvantage of tyranny and superstition grounded into our principles as was beyond the manhood of a Roman recovery,[10] it will be attributed first, as is most due, to the strong assistance of God, our deliverer; next, to your faithful guidance and undaunted wisdom, Lords and Commons of England. Neither is it, in God's esteem, the diminution of His glory, when honorable things are spoken of good men and worthy magistrates; which if I now first should begin to do, after so fair a progress of your laudable deeds, and such a long obligement upon the whole realm to your indefatigable virtues, I might be justly reckoned among the tardiest and the unwillingest of them that praise ye.

Nevertheless, there being three principal things without which all praising is but courtship and flattery: first, when that only is praised which is solidly worth praise; next, when greatest likelihoods are brought that such things are truly and really in those persons to whom they are ascribed; the other, when he who praises, by showing that such his actual persuasion is of whom he writes, can demonstrate that he flatters not; the former two of these I have heretofore

---

[8] Which . . . liberty though I confess at once this feeling, I shall be blameless if it is only the joy and gratulation that wishing to promote their country's liberty brings to all who do wish to promote it   [9] trophy memorial of victory: the discourse will be a testimony to my desire to promote liberty, even if it is not successful   [10] steep . . . recovery we had fallen as low in tyranny and superstition as the Romans, who could not rise from their decline and fall, yet we did recover

endeavored, rescuing the employment from him[11] who went about to impair your merits with a trivial and malignant encomium; the latter, as belonging chiefly to mine own acquittal, that whom I so extolled I did not flatter, hath been reserved opportunely to this occasion. For he who freely magnifies what hath been nobly done, and fears not to declare as freely what might be done better, gives ye the best covenant of his fidelity, and that his loyalest affection and his hope waits on your proceedings. His highest praising is not flattery, and his plainest advice is a kind of praising; for though I should affirm and hold by argument that it would fare better with truth, with learning, and the commonwealth, if one of your published orders, which I should name, were called in, yet at the same time it could not but much redound to the lustre of your mild and equal [12] government, whenas private persons are hereby animated to think ye better pleased with public advice than other statists[13] have been delighted heretofore with public flattery. And men will then see what difference there is between the magnanimity of a triennial [14] parliament and that jealous haughtiness of prelates and cabin[15] counsellors that usurped of late, whenas they shall observe ye in the midst of your victories and successes more gently brooking written exceptions against a voted order than other courts, which had produced nothing worth memory but the weak ostentation of wealth, would have endured the least signified dislike at any sudden proclamation.

If I should thus far presume upon the meek demeanor of your civil and gentle greatness, Lords and Commons, as

[11] him . . . encomium Joseph Hall, whose *Humble Remonstrance to the High Court of Parliament* (1641) started the controversy over episcopalianism in which Milton had taken part. Milton argues that Hall was merely a flatterer, since his praise of Parliament was trivial (commonplace) and malignant (favorable to the King)   [12] equal just   [13] statists statesmen   [14] triennial an act passed in 1641 provided that Parliament should meet at least once in three years   [15] cabin a political cabinet; referring especially to the Cabinet Council and the extraordinary courts of Star Chamber and High Commission in which the King had been accustomed to transact public business in private session with a few favorites

what your published order hath directly said that to gain-
say, I might defend myself with ease, if any should accuse
me of being new[16] or insolent, did they but know how much
better I find ye esteem it to imitate the old and elegant
humanity of Greece than the barbaric pride of a Hunnish
and Norwegian stateliness. And out of those ages, to whose
polite wisdom and letters we owe that we are not yet[17]
Goths and Jutlanders, I could name him[18] who from his
private house wrote that discourse to the parliament of
Athens, that persuades[19] them to change the form of de-
mocracy which was then established. Such honor was done
in those days to men who professed the study of wisdom
and eloquence, not only in their own country but in other
lands, that cities and seignories heard them gladly and with
great respect, if they had aught in public to admonish the
state. Thus did Dion Prusæus, a stranger and a private
orator, counsel the Rhodians against a former edict: and I
abound with other like examples, which to set here would
be superfluous. But if from the industry of a life wholly
dedicated to studious labors, and those natural endowments
haply not the worst[20] for two and fifty degrees of northern
latitude, so much must be derogated [21] as to count me not
equal to any of those who had this privilege, I would obtain
to be thought not so inferior as yourselves are superior to
the most of them who received their counsel: and how far
you excel them, be assured, Lords and Commons, there
can no greater testimony appear than when your prudent
spirit acknowledges and obeys the voice of reason, from
what quarter soever it be heard speaking, and renders ye
as willing to repeal any act of your own setting forth as any
set forth by your predecessors.

If ye be thus resolved, as it were injury to think ye were
not, I know not what should withhold me from presenting

---

[16] new presumptuous   [17] yet still   [18] him Isocrates; see note to
the title, p. 1   [19] persuades urges   [20] worst . . . counsel though
my endowments—not the worst in England with its northern
climate—are not equal to those of the southern orators mentioned, my inferiority is more than made up by your superiority
to those whom they addressed   [21] derogated subtracted

ye with a fit instance wherein to show both that love of
truth which ye eminently profess, and that uprightness of
your judgment which is not wont to be partial to yourselves,
by judging over again that Order which ye have ordained
"to regulate printing: that no book, pamphlet, or paper shall
be henceforth printed, unless the same be first approved
and licensed by such, or at least one of such, as shall be
thereto appointed." For that part which preserves justly
every man's copy[22] to himself, or provides for the poor, I
touch not; only wish they be not made pretences to abuse
and persecute honest and painful [23] men, who offend not
in either of these particulars. But that other clause of licensing books, which we thought had died with his brother
quadragesimal and matrimonial [24] when the prelates ex-
pired, I shall now attend [25] with such a homily as shall lay
before ye, first, the inventors of it to be those whom ye will
be loath to own; next, what is to be thought in general of
reading, whatever sort the books be; and that this Order
avails nothing to the suppressing of scandalous, seditious,
and libellous books, which were mainly intended to be
suppressed. Last, that it will be primely to the discouragement of all learning, and the stop of truth, not only by
disexercising and blunting our abilities in what we know
already, but by hindering and cropping the discovery that
might be yet further made, both in religious and civil
wisdom.

I deny not but that it is of greatest concernment in the
church and commonwealth, to have a vigilant eye how
books demean themselves as well as men; and thereafter to
confine, imprison, and do sharpest justice on them as male-
factors: for books are not absolutely dead things, but do
contain a potency of life in them to be as active as that soul
was whose progeny they are; nay, they do preserve as in a
vial the purest efficacy and extraction of that living intellect
that bred them. I know they are as lively, and as vigorously

[22] copy copyright    [23] painful painstaking    [24] quadragesimal . . .
matrimonial a dispensation from fasting in Lent and a marriage-
license issued by the church; Milton regarded marriage as a civil
contract    [25] attend turn my attention to

productive, as those fabulous dragon's teeth; and being sown up and down, may chance to spring up armed men. And yet, on the other hand, unless wariness be used, as good almost kill a man as kill a good book: who kills a man kills a reasonable creature, God's image; but he who destroys a good book, kills reason itself, kills the image of God, as it were, in the eye.[26] Many a man lives a burden to the earth; but a good book is the precious life-blood of a master-spirit, embalmed and treasured up on purpose to a life beyond life. 'Tis true, no age can restore a life, whereof, perhaps, there is no great loss; and revolutions of ages do not oft recover the loss of a rejected truth, for the want of which whole nations fare the worse. We should be wary therefore what persecution we raise against the living labors of public men, how we spill [27] that seasoned life of man, preserved and stored up in books; since we see a kind of homicide may be thus committed, sometimes a martyrdom; and if it extend to the whole impression, a kind of massacre, whereof the execution ends not in the slaying of an elemental life, but strikes at that ethereal and fifth essence,[28] the breath of reason itself; slays an immortality rather than a life. But lest I should be condemned of introducing license while I oppose licensing, I refuse not the pains to be so much historical as will serve to show what hath been done by ancient and famous commonwealths against this disorder, till the very time that this project of licensing crept out of the Inquisition,[29] was catched up by our prelates, and hath caught some of our presbyters.

In Athens, where books and wits were ever busier than

[26] kills . . . eye strikes in a vital spot   [27] spill destroy   [28] elemental . . . essence contrasting the four earthly elements (earth, water, air, and fire) with the fifth or heavenly essence (ether)   [29] Inquisition the jurisdiction of the church over heresy, or the holding of beliefs contrary to accepted teaching. Milton argues, correctly, that the Anglican bishops formerly, and now the Presbyterians, seek to retain a power exercised by the Roman Church. With his highly prejudiced history cf. the *Encyclopaedia Brittanica* or the *Encyclopaedia of the Social Sciences, s.v.* Inquisition

in any other part of Greece, I find but only two sorts of writings which the magistrate cared to take notice of: those either blasphemous and atheistical, or libellous. Thus the books of Protagoras were by the judges of Areopagus commanded to be burnt, and himself banished the territory, for a discourse begun with his confessing not to know "whether there were gods or whether not." And against defaming, it was decreed that none should be traduced by name, as was the manner of Vetus Comœdia,[30] whereby we may guess how they censured libelling; and this course was quick[31] enough, as Cicero writes, to quell both the desperate wits of other atheists and the open way of defaming, as the event showed. Of other sects and opinions, though tending to voluptuousness and the denying of divine Providence, they took no heed. Therefore we do not read that either Epicurus, or that libertine school of Cyrene,[32] or what the Cynic impudence[33] uttered, was ever questioned by the laws. Neither is it recorded that the writings of those old comedians were suppressed, though the acting of them were forbid; and that Plato commended the reading of Aristophanes, the loosest of them all, to his royal scholar Dionysius, is commonly known, and may be excused, if holy Chrysostom,[34] as is reported, nightly studied so much the same author, and had the art to cleanse a scurrilous vehemence into the style of a rousing sermon.

That other leading city of Greece, Lacedæmon, considering that Lycurgus[35] their lawgiver was so addicted to elegant learning as to have been the first that brought out of Ionia the scattered works of Homer, and sent the poet Thales from Crete to prepare and mollify the Spartan

[30] Vetus Comoedia early Greek comedy (second half of the fifth century B.C.), which permitted the broadest personalities in political satire   [31] quick vigorous   [32] Epicurus . . . Cyrene both schools taught that the end of life is to enjoy pleasure, and the Epicureans believed that the gods are indifferent to human affairs   [33] impudence the Cynics were noted for the insolence of their manners   [34] Chrysostom St. John Chrysostom (c. 347-407), noted for his eloquence   [35] Lycurgus an almost mythical figure; Milton follows mainly the biography in Plutarch's *Lives*

surliness with his smooth songs and odes, the better to
plant among them law and civility, it is to be wondered
how museless and unbookish they were, minding nought
but the feats of war. There needed no licensing of books
among them, for they disliked all but their own laconic
apothegms,[36] and took a slight occasion to chase Archilo-
chus out of their city, perhaps for composing in a higher
strain than their own soldierly ballads and roundels[37] could
reach to; or if it were for his broad verses, they were not
therein so cautious but they were as dissolute in their pro-
miscuous conversing;[38] whence Euripides affirms, in *An-
dromache,* that their women were all unchaste. Thus much
may give us light after what sort[39] books were prohibited
among the Greeks.

The Romans also, for many ages trained up only to a military roughness, resembling most the Lacedæmonian guise,
knew of learning little but what their Twelve Tables[40]
and the Pontific College with their augurs and flamens[41]
taught them in religion and law; so unacquainted with other
learning that when Carneades and Critolaus, with the Stoic
Diogenes, coming ambassadors[42] to Rome, took thereby
occasion to give the city a taste of their philosophy, they
were suspected for seducers by no less a man than Cato the
Censor, who moved it in the Senate to dismiss them speedily, and to banish all such Attic babblers out of Italy. But
Scipio and others of the noblest senators withstood him and
his old Sabine austerity; honored and admired the men;
and the censor himself at last, in his old age, fell to the
study of that whereof before he was so scrupulous. And yet
at the same time Nævius and Plautus, the first Latin comedians, had filled the city with all the borrowed scenes of

[36] apothegms short maxims called laconic because of the Spartan
fondness for them  [37] roundel song to accompany a round dance
[38] conversing association  [39] after what sort in what manner
[40] Twelve Tables a Roman legal code of the fifth century B.C.
[41] Pontific . . . flamens the chief body of the Roman priesthood
with two subordinate classes of priests  [42] ambassadors in 155
B.C. The three philosophers mentioned were the heads of the
three principal Athenian schools

Menander and Philemon.[43] Then began to be considered
there also what was to be done to libellous books and
authors; for Nævius was quickly cast into prison for his
unbridled pen, and released by the tribunes upon his
recantation: we read also that libels were burnt, and the
makers punished, by Augustus.

The like severity, no doubt, was used if aught were
impiously written against their esteemed gods. Except in
these two points, how the world went in books the magistrate kept no reckoning. And therefore Lucretius,[44] without
impeachment, versifies his Epicurism to Memmius, and had
the honor to be set forth the second time by Cicero, so great
a father of the commonwealth; although himself disputes
against that opinion in his own writings. Nor was the satirical sharpness or naked plainness of Lucilius,[45] or Catullus,
or Flaccus,[46] by any order prohibited. And for matters of
state, the story[47] of Titus Livius, though it extolled that
part which Pompey held,[48] was not therefore suppressed
by Octavius Cæsar of the other faction. But that Naso[49]
was by him banished in his old age, for the wanton poems
of his youth, was but a mere covert of state over some
secret cause; and besides, the books were neither banished
nor called in. From hence[50] we shall meet with little else
but tyranny in the Roman empire, that we may not marvel
if not so often bad as good books were silenced. I shall
therefore deem to have been large enough in producing
what among the ancients was punishable to write, save
only which all other arguments were free to treat on.

[43] Menander . . . Philemon Greek comedy-writers of the fourth
century B.C., imitated by the Latin dramatists mentioned
[44] Lucretius His poem On the Nature of Things set forth
Epicurus's philosophy and attacked religion as the chief source
of superstitious fears. It is reported to have been edited by
Cicero, though not for a "second time" as Milton says  [45] Lucilius . . . Flaccus Latin satirical poets  [46] Flaccus Horace
[47] story history  [48] part . . . held the side that Pompey took
[49] Naso Ovid, banished by Augustus, A.D. 9  [50] from hence from
the time of Augustus; any censorship in the first three Christian
centuries is to be set down to the despotism of the time

By this time the emperors were become Christians, whose discipline in this point I do not find to have been more severe than what was formerly in practice. The books of those whom they took to be grand heretics were examined, refuted, and condemned in the general councils; and not till then were prohibited, or burnt, by authority of the emperor. As for the writings of heathen authors, unless they were plain invectives against Christianity, as those of Porphyrius and Proclus,[51] they met with no interdict that can be cited, till about the year 400 in a Carthaginian Council, wherein bishops themselves were forbid to read the books of Gentiles,[52] but heresies they might read; while others long before them, on the contrary, scrupled more the books of heretics than of Gentiles. And that the primitive councils and bishops were wont only to declare what books were not commendable, passing no further but leaving it to each one's conscience to read or to lay by, till after the year 800, is observed already by Padre Paolo,[53] the great unmasker of the Trentine Council. After which time[54] the Popes of Rome, engrossing[55] what they pleased of political rule into their own hands, extended their dominion over men's eyes, as they had before over their judgments, burning and prohibiting to be read what they fancied not; yet sparing in their censures, and the books not many which they dealt with; till Martin V,[56] by his bull, not only prohibited, but was the first that excommunicated [57] the reading of heretical books; for about that time Wyclif [58] and

[51] Porphyrius . . . Proclus Neoplatonists and so enemies of Christianity [52] Gentiles heathens [53] Padre Paolo . . . Council Paolo Sarpi (1552-1623) theological adviser to the Republic of Venice in its controversy with Pope Paul V, exponent of the control of the state over the clergy in all secular matters, and historian of the Council of Trent. This Council (1545-1563), though called in the hope that it might reconcile the differences between Protestants and Catholics, affirmed the supremacy of the Pope in the church and so made the breach irreparable [54] which time 800 [55] engrossing monopolizing [56] Martin V pope 1417-1431 [57] excommunicated forbade on pain of excommunication [58] Wyclif John (c. 1324-1384) English reformer and critic of the papacy

Huss[59] growing terrible, were they who first drove the Papal Court to a stricter policy of prohibiting. Which course Leo X and his successors followed, until the Council of Trent and the Spanish Inquisition, engendering together, brought forth or perfected those catalogues and expurging indexes[60] that rake through the entrails of many an old good author with a violation worse than any could be offered to his tomb.

Nor did they stay in matters heretical, but any subject that was not to their palate they either condemned in a prohibition, or had it straight into the new purgatory of an index. To fill up the measure of encroachment, their last invention was to ordain that no book, pamphlet, or paper should be printed (as if St. Peter had bequeathed them the keys of the press also out of Paradise) unless it were approved and licensed under the hands of two or three glutton friars. For example:

> Let the Chancellor Cini be pleased to see if in this present work be contained aught that may withstand the printing.
> > *Vincent Rabatta,* Vicar of Florence.
> I have seen this present work, and find nothing athwart the Catholic faith and good manners: in witness whereof I have given, &c.
> > *Nicolo Cini,* Chancellor of Florence.
> Attending the precedent relation, it is allowed that this present work of Davanzati may be printed.
> > Vincent Rabatta, &c.

It may be printed, July 15.
> *Friar Simon Mompei d'Amelia,*
> Chancellor of the Holy Office in Florence.

Sure they have a conceit, if he of the bottomless pit had not long since broke prison, that this quadruple exorcism would bar him down. I fear their next design will be to get

---

[59] Huss John (c. 1373-1415) Czech reformer and disciple of Wyclif, burned at the stake, 1415  [60] catalogues . . . indexes of books that are prohibited and of those that may be read only after expurgation

into their custody the licensing of that which they say
Claudius* intended but went not through with. Vouchsafe
to see another of their forms, the Roman stamp:

Imprimatur,[61] If it seem good to the reverend Master of
the Holy Palace,

*Belcastro,* Vicegerent.

Imprimatur,

*Friar Nicolo Rodolphi,*
Master of the Holy Palace.

Sometimes five imprimaturs are seen together, dialogue-
wise, in the piazza of one title-page, complimenting and
ducking each to other with their shaven reverences, whether
the author, who stands by in perplexity at the foot of his
epistle, shall to the press or to the sponge. These are the
pretty responsories, these are the dear antiphonies, that so
bewitched of late our prelates and their chaplains, with the
goodly echo they made, and besotted us to the gay imitation of a lordly imprimatur, one from Lambeth House, another from the west end of Paul's;[62] so apishly Romanising
that the word of command still was set down in Latin, as if
the learned grammatical pen that wrote it would cast no
ink without Latin; or perhaps, as they thought, because no
vulgar tongue was worthy to express the pure conceit[63] of
an imprimatur; but rather, as I hope, for that our English,
the language of men ever famous and foremost in the
achievements of liberty, will not easily find servile letters
enow to spell such a dictatory presumption English.[64]

And thus ye have the inventors and the original of book-
licensing ripped up[65] and drawn as lineally as any pedigree.
We have it not, that can be heard of, from any ancient state,

* Quo veniam daret flatum crepitumque ventris in convivio
emittendi. Sueton. in Claudio. [Milton's note]

[61] imprimatur it may be printed   [62] Lambeth House . . . Paul's
the official residences in London respectively of the Archbishop
of Canterbury and the Bishop of London, the ecclesiastical authorities that had usually been entrusted with licensing books
[63] conceit idea   [64] English in English   [65] ripped up disclosed

or polity, or church, nor by any statute left us by our ancestors elder or later; nor from the modern custom of any reformed city or church abroad; but from the most antichristian council and the most tyrannous inquisition that
ever inquired. Till then books were ever as freely admitted
into the world as any other birth; the issue of the brain was
no more stifled than the issue of the womb: no envious
Juno[66] sat cross-legged over the nativity of any man's intellectual offspring; but if it proved a monster, who denies but
that it was justly burnt or sunk into the sea? But that a
book, in worse condition[67] than a peccant soul, should be to
stand before a jury ere it be born to the world, and undergo
yet in darkness the judgment of Radamanth and his col-
leagues, ere it can pass the ferry backward into light, was
never heard before, till that mysterious iniquity,[68] provoked
and troubled at the first entrance of reformation, sought out
new limboes and new hells wherein they might include our
books also within the number of their damned. And this
was the rare morsel so officiously snatched up, and so ill-
favoredly imitated by our inquisiturient[69] bishops and the
attendant minorites[70] their chaplains. That ye like not now
these most certain authors of this licensing order, and that
all sinister intention was far distant from your thoughts
when ye were importuned the passing it, all men who know
the integrity of your actions, and how ye honor truth, will
clear ye readily.

But some will say, what though the inventors were bad,
the thing for all that may be good. It may so; yet if that
thing be no such deep invention, but obvious and easy for
any man to light on, and yet best and wisest commonwealths through all ages and occasions have forborne to use
it, and falsest seducers and oppressors of men were the first

---

[66] Juno because of jealousy she tried by her spells to prevent the
birth of Hercules  [67] worse condition souls were judged after
death for sins committed but books are to be judged before birth
[68] mysterious iniquity the woman of *Revelation* xvii, identified by
Protestant reformers with the papacy  [69] inquisiturient eager to
play the inquisitor  [70] minorites persons of minor rank; licensing
had commonly been deputed by the bishops to their chaplains

who took it up, and to no other purpose but to obstruct and hinder the first approach of reformation, I am of those who believe it will be a harder alchemy than Lullius[71] ever knew, to sublimate[72] any good use out of such an invention. Yet this only is what I request to gain from this reason, that it may be held a dangerous and suspicious fruit, as certainly it deserves, for the tree that bore it, until I can dissect one by one the properties it has. But I have first to finish, as was propounded, what is to be thought in general of reading books, whatever sort they be, and whether be more the benefit or the harm that thence proceeds.

Not to insist upon the examples of Moses, Daniel, and Paul, who were skilful in all the learning of the Egyptians, Chaldeans, and Greeks, which could not probably be without reading their books of all sorts, in[73] Paul especially, who thought it no defilement to insert into Holy Scripture the sentences[74] of three Greek poets, and one of them a tragedian; the question was notwithstanding sometimes controverted among the primitive doctors, but with great odds on that side which affirmed it both lawful and profitable, as was then evidently perceived when Julian[75] the Apostate, and subtlest enemy to our faith, made a decree forbidding Christians the study of heathen learning; for, said he, they wound us with our own weapons, and with our own arts and sciences they overcome us. And indeed the Christians were put so to their shifts by this crafty means, and so much in danger to decline into all ignorance, that the two Apollinarii[76] were fain, as a man may say, to coin all the seven liberal sciences out of the Bible, reducing it into divers forms of orations, poems, dialogues, even to the calculating of a new Christian grammar. But, saith the historian Soc-

[71] **Lullius** Raymond (c. 1235-1315) logician, missionary, and student of Arabic, reputed (on insufficient evidence) to have been an alchemist  [72] sublimate extract  [73] in in the case of [74] sentences sayings: *Acts* xvii, 28 (from Aratus); *I Corinthians* xv, 33 (from Euripides); *Titus* i, 12 (from Epimenides) [75] Julian Emperor, 361-363, excluded Christians from the schools [76] Apollonarii Christian rhetoricians who rewrote the Bible as described

rates,[77] the providence of God provided better than the industry of Apollinarius and his son, by taking away that illiterate law with the life of him who devised it.

So great an injury they then held it to be deprived of Hellenic learning; and thought it a persecution more undermining, and secretly decaying the church, than the open cruelty of Decius or Diocletian.[78] And perhaps it was [with] the same politic drift that the devil whipped St. Jerome[79] in a Lenten dream for reading Cicero; or else it was a phantasm bred by the fever which had then seized him. For had an angel been his discipliner, unless it were for dwelling too much upon Ciceronianisms,[80] and had chastised the reading, not the vanity, it had been plainly partial, first, to correct him for grave Cicero and not for scurril Plautus, whom he confesses to have been reading not long before; next, to correct him only, and let so many more ancient fathers wax old in those pleasant and florid studies, without the lash of such a tutoring apparition; insomuch that Basil [81] teaches how some good use may be made of Margites,[82] a sportful poem, not now extant, writ by Homer; and why not then of Morgante,[83] an Italian romance much to the same purpose?

But if it be agreed we shall be tried by visions, there is a vision recorded by Eusebius,[84] far ancienter than this tale[85] of Jerome to the nun Eustochium, and besides, has nothing of a fever in it. Dionysius Alexandrinus was, about the year 240, a person of great name in the church for piety and learning, who had wont[86] to avail himself much against heretics by being conversant in their books, until a certain presbyter laid it scrupulously to his conscience, how he durst venture himself among those defiling volumes. The

[77] Socrates church historian of the fifth century    [78] Decius . . . Diocletian emperors whose reigns were notable for persecution [79] St. Jerome c. 340-420, translator of the Bible into Latin [80] Ciceronianisms niceties of Latin style copied from Cicero [81] Basil Bishop of Caesarea, 370-379    [82] Margites Milton follows Aristotle's account of it; *Poetics* 1448 b 39    [83] Morgante a mock-romantic poem by Luigi Pulci published in Venice, 1481 [84] Eusebius *Church History*, VII, 7    [85] tale i.e., the one preceding, which occurs in a letter of Jerome to Eustochium    [86] had wont was accustomed

worthy man, loath to give offence,[87] fell into a new debate
with himself what was to be thought; when suddenly a vision sent from God (it is his own epistle that so avers it)
confirmed him in these words: "Read any books whatever
come to thy hands, for thou art sufficient both to judge
aright and to examine each matter." To this revelation he
assented the sooner, as he confesses, because it was answerable to that of the Apostle to the Thessalonians: "Prove all
things, hold fast that which is good."

And he might have added another remarkable saying of
the same author: "To the pure all things are pure;" not only
meats and drinks, but all kind of knowledge whether of
good or evil; the knowledge cannot defile, nor consequently
the books, if the will and conscience be not defiled. For
books are as meats and viands are, some of good, some of
evil substance; and yet God in that unapocryphal vision said
without exception, "Rise, Peter, kill and eat," leaving the
choice to each man's discretion. Wholesome meats to a
vitiated stomach differ little or nothing from unwholesome;
and best books to a naughty mind are not unappliable to
occasions of evil. Bad meats will scarce breed good nourish-
ment in the healthiest concoction;[88] but herein the difference is of bad books, that they to a discreet and judicious
reader serve in many respects to discover, to confute, to
forewarn, and to illustrate. Whereof what better witness can
ye expect I should produce than one of your own now sitting in Parliament, the chief of learned men reputed in this
land, Mr. Selden,[89] whose volume of natural and national
laws proves, not only by great authorities brought together,
but by exquisite[90] reasons and theorems almost mathemati-
cally demonstrative, that all opinions, yea, errors, known,
read, and collated, are of main service and assistance toward the speedy attainment of what is truest.

[87] give offence cause anyone to stumble  [88] concoction digestion
[89] Selden John (1584-1654) was not only the greatest scholar
then living in England but also one of the boldest thinkers. His
views on intellectual freedom were similar to Milton's. The book
mentioned is his *De jure naturali et gentium juxta disciplinam
Ebraeorum*, 1640  [90] exquisite well selected

I conceive therefore that when God did enlarge the universal diet of man's body (saving ever the rules of temperance), he then also, as before, left arbitrary the dieting and repasting of our minds; as wherein every mature man might have to exercise his own leading capacity. How great a virtue is temperance, how much of moment through the whole life of man! Yet God commits the managing so great a trust, without particular law or prescription, wholly to the demeanor[91] of every grown man. And therefore, when he himself tabled the Jews from heaven, that omer, which was every man's daily portion of manna, is computed to have been more than might have well sufficed the heartiest feeder thrice as many meals. For those actions which enter into a man, rather than issue out of him, and therefore defile not, God uses not to captivate under a perpetual childhood of prescription, but trusts him with the gift of reason to be his own chooser; there were but little work left for preaching, if law and compulsion should grow so fast upon those things which heretofore were governed only by exhortation. Solomon informs us that much reading is a weariness to the flesh; but neither he nor other inspired author tells us that such or such reading is unlawful: yet certainly had God thought good to limit us herein, it had been much more expedient to have told us what was unlawful than what was wearisome.

As for the burning of those Ephesian books by St. Paul's converts, 'tis replied the books were magic, the Syriac so renders them. It was a private act, a voluntary act, and leaves us to a voluntary imitation: the men in remorse burnt those books which were their own; the magistrate by this example is not appointed;[92] these men practised the books, another might perhaps have read them in some sort usefully.

Good and evil we know in the field of this world grow up together almost inseparably; and the knowledge of good is so involved and interwoven with the knowledge of evil, and in so many cunning resemblances hardly to be discerned, that those confused seeds which were imposed upon

[91] **demeanor** management　　[92] **appointed** determined

Psyche[93] as an incessant labor to cull out and sort asunder, were not more intermixed. It was from out the rind of one apple tasted that the knowledge of good and evil, as two twins cleaving together, leaped forth into the world. And perhaps this is that doom which Adam fell into of knowing good and evil, that is to say, of knowing good by evil.

As therefore the state of man now is, what wisdom can there be to choose, what continence to forbear, without the knowledge of evil? He that can apprehend and consider vice with all her baits and seeming pleasures, and yet abstain, and yet distinguish, and yet prefer that which is truly better, he is the true wayfaring[94] Christian. I cannot praise a fugitive and cloistered virtue, unexercised and unbreathed, that never sallies out and sees her adversary, but slinks out of the race, where that immortal garland is to be run for, not without dust and heat. Assuredly we bring not innocence into the world, we bring impurity much rather: that which purifies us is trial, and trial is by what is contrary. That virtue therefore which is but a youngling in the contemplation of evil, and knows not the utmost that vice promises to her followers, and rejects it, is but a blank virtue, not a pure; her whiteness is but an excremental [95] whiteness; which was the reason why our sage and serious poet Spenser (whom I dare be known to think a better teacher than Scotus or Aquinas[96]), describing true temperance under the person of Guion, brings him in with his palmer through the cave of Mammon and the bower of earthly bliss, that he might see and know, and yet abstain.

Since therefore the knowledge and survey of vice is in this world so necessary to the constituting of human virtue, and the scanning of error to the confirmation of truth, how can we more safely and with less danger scout into the

[93] Venus, being jealous of Cupid's love for Psyche, mixed together many kinds of small seeds and required her to sort them out before sundown. The ants performed the task for her. See Apuleius, *The Golden Ass,* Book VI.   [94] wayfaring Milton probably wrote warfaring   [95] excremental superficial   [96] Scotus . . . Aquinas founders of the principal and rival schools of medieval philosophy

regions of sin and falsity than by reading all manner of tractates, and hearing all manner of reason? And this is the benefit which may be had of books promiscuously read.

But of the harm that may result hence three kinds are usually reckoned. First, is feared the infection that may spread; but then, all human learning and controversy in religious points must remove out of the world, yea, the Bible itself; for that ofttimes relates blasphemy not nicely,[97] it describes the carnal sense of wicked men not unelegantly, it brings in holiest men passionately murmuring against Providence through all the arguments of Epicurus: in other great disputes it answers dubiously and darkly to the common reader: and ask a Talmudist what ails the modesty of his marginal Keri, that Moses and all the prophets cannot persuade him to pronounce the textual Chetiv.[98] For these causes we all know the Bible itself put by the papist into the first rank of prohibited books. The ancientest fathers must be next removed, as Clement of Alexandria, and that Eusebian book of evangelic preparation transmitting our ears through a hoard of heathenish obscenities to receive the Gospel. Who finds not that Irenæus, Epiphanius, Jerome,[99] and others discover[1] more heresies than they well confute, and that oft for heresy which is the truer opinion?

Nor boots it to say for these, and all the heathen writers of greatest infection, if it must be thought so, with whom is bound up the life of human learning, that they writ in an unknown tongue, so long as we are sure those languages are known as well to the worst of men, who are both most able and most diligent to instil the poison they suck, first into the courts of princes, acquainting them with the choicest de-

[97] nicely squeamishly  [98] Keri . . . Chetiv a gloss put in the margin to be read (keri) in place of the word written (chetiv) in the text, when the latter was deemed too coarse to be spoken. The Talmud is a body of Jewish civil and religious law with commentary  [99] Clement . . . Jerome church fathers, of whom Clement and Eusebius write especially of the relation between Christianity and paganism, and the other three of heresies among the Christians  [1] discover uncover

lights and criticisms[2] of sin. As perhaps did that Petronius, whom Nero called his Arbiter, the master of his revels; and that notorious ribald [3] of Arezzo, dreaded and yet dear to the Italian courtiers. I name not him, for posterity's sake,[4] whom Harry VIII named in merriment his vicar of hell. By which compendious way all the contagion that foreign books can infuse will find a passage to the people far easier and shorter than an Indian voyage, though it could be sailed either by the north of Cathay eastward, or of Canada westward, while our Spanish licensing gags the English press never so severely.

But on the other side, that infection which is from books of controversy in religion is more doubtful and dangerous to the learned than to the ignorant; and yet those books must be permitted untouched by the licenser. It will be hard to instance where any ignorant man hath been ever seduced by papistical book in English, unless it were commended and expounded to him by some of that clergy; and indeed all such tractates, whether false or true, are as the prophecy of Isaiah was to the eunuch, not to be "understood without a guide." But of our priests and doctors how many have been corrupted by studying the comments of Jesuits and Sorbonists,[5] and how fast they could transfuse that corruption into the people, our experience is both late and sad. It is not forgot, since the acute and distinct[6] Arminius[7] was perverted merely by the perusing of a nameless[8] discourse written at Delft, which at first he took in hand to confute.

Seeing therefore that those books, and those in great abundance, which are likeliest to taint both life and doctrine, cannot be suppressed without the fall of learning and of all ability in disputation, and that these books of either sort are most and soonest catching to the learned (from

[2] criticisms refinements  [3] ribald Pietro Aretino (1492-1557)  [4] him . . . sake reference unknown; presumably the person meant had living descendants  [5] Sorbonists the Sorbonne in Paris was the principal school of Roman Catholic theology  [6] distinct clear-headed  [7] Arminius a Dutch Calvinist theologian whose belief in predestination was thus upset  [8] nameless anonymous

whom to the common people whatever is heretical or dissolute may quickly be conveyed), and that evil manners are as perfectly learned without books a thousand other ways which cannot be stopped, and evil doctrine not with books can propagate except a teacher guide, which he might also do without writing and so beyond prohibiting, I am not able to unfold how this cautelous[9] enterprise of licensing can be exempted from the number of vain and impossible attempts. And he who were pleasantly disposed could not well avoid to liken it to the exploit of that gallant man who thought to pound up the crows by shutting his park gate.

Besides another inconvenience, if learned men be the first receivers out of books and dispreaders both of vice and error, how shall the licensers themselves be confided in, unless we can confer upon them, or they assume to themselves above all others in the land, the grace of infallibility and uncorruptedness? And again, if it be true that a wise man like a good refiner can gather gold out of the drossiest volume, and that a fool will be a fool with the best book, yea, or without book, there is no reason that we should deprive a wise man of any advantage to his wisdom, while we seek to restrain from a fool that which being restrained will be no hindrance to his folly. For if there should be so much exactness always used to keep that from him which is unfit for his reading, we should in the judgment of Aristotle not only, but of Solomon and of our Saviour, not vouchsafe him good precepts, and by consequence not willingly admit him to good books; as being certain that a wise man will make better use of an idle pamphlet than a fool will do of sacred Scripture.

'Tis next alleged we must not expose ourselves to temptations without necessity, and next to that, not employ our time in vain things. To both these objections one answer will serve, out of the grounds already laid, that to all men such books are not temptations nor vanities, but useful drugs and materials wherewith to temper and compose effective and strong medicines, which man's life cannot

[9] cautelous deceitful

want.[10] The rest, as children and childish men, who have
not the art to qualify[11] and prepare these working minerals,
well may be exhorted to forbear, but hindered forcibly they
cannot be by all the licensing that sainted Inquisition could
ever yet contrive; which is what I promised to deliver next:
that this order of licensing conduces nothing to the end for
which it was framed; and hath almost prevented [12] me by
being clear already while thus much hath been explaining.
See the ingenuity[13] of Truth, who, when she gets a free and
willing hand, opens herself faster than the pace of method
and discourse[14] can overtake her.

It was the task which I began with to show that no nation
or well instituted state, if they valued books at all, did ever
use this way of licensing; and it might be answered that this
is a piece of prudence lately discovered. To which I return,
that as it was a thing slight and obvious to think on, so if it
had been difficult to find out, there wanted not among them
long since who suggested such a course; which they not fol-
lowing, leave us a pattern of their judgment that it was not
the not knowing, but the not approving, which was the
cause of their not using it.

Plato, a man of high authority indeed, but least of all for
his commonwealth, in the book of his laws, which no city
ever yet received, fed his fancy with making many edicts to
his airy burgomasters,[15] which they who otherwise admire
him wish had been rather buried and excused in the genial
cups of an Academic night sitting. By which laws[16] he
seems to tolerate no kind of learning but by unalterable
decree, consisting most of practical traditions, to the attainment whereof a library of smaller bulk than his own dialogues would be abundant. And there also enacts that no
poet should so much as read to any private man what he
had written, until the judges and law-keepers had seen it

---

[10] want be without  [11] qualify modify or control  [12] prevented
outrun  [13] ingenuity candor or frankness  [14] discourse reason
[15] airy burgomasters imaginary magistrates  [16] laws Milton seems
to have in mind *Laws* 811 D, 801 D. See Book VII *passim;* cf.
*Republic,* Book III

and allowed it; but that Plato meant this law peculiarly to
that commonwealth which he had imagined, and to no
other, is evident. Why was he not else a lawgiver to himself,
but a transgressor, and to be expelled by his own magistrates, both for the wanton epigrams and dialogues which
he made, and his perpetual reading of Sophron Mimus[17]
and Aristophanes, books of grossest infamy; and also for
commending the latter of them, though he were the malicious libeller[18] of his chief friends, to be read by the tyrant
Dionysius, who had little need of such trash to spend his
time on?—but that he knew this licensing of poems had
reference and dependence to many other provisoes there set
down in his fancied republic, which in this world could
have no place; and so neither he himself, nor any magistrate or city, ever imitated that course, which, taken apart
from those other collateral injunctions, must needs be vain
and fruitless.

For if they fell upon[19] one kind of strictness, unless their
care were equal to regulate all other things of like aptness
to corrupt the mind, that single endeavor they knew would
be but a fond [20] labor: to shut and fortify one gate against
corruption, and be necessitated to leave others round about
wide open. If we think to regulate printing, thereby to rec-
tify manners, we must regulate all recreations and pastimes,
all that is delightful to man. No music must be heard, no
song be set or sung, but what is grave and Doric. There
must be licensing dancers, that no gesture, motion, or de-
portment be taught our youth, but what by their allowance
shall be thought honest; for such Plato was provided of.[21]
It will ask more than the work of twenty licensers to examine all the lutes, the violins, and the guitars in every
house; they must not be suffered to prattle as they do, but

---

[17] Sophron Sicilian writer of mimes, i.e., comedies not intended
for stage-production presenting, often humorously, scenes of
daily life  [18] libeller of Socrates in the *Clouds*  [19] fell upon
adopted  [20] fond foolish  [21] Plato . . . of if books are to be
licensed, so must music and all forms of recreation and education, as in Plato's *Republic* and *Laws*

must be licensed what they may say. And who shall silence all the airs and madrigals that whisper softness in chambers? The windows also, and the balconies, must be thought on; there are shrewd [22] books, with dangerous frontispieces, set to sale: who shall prohibit them, shall twenty licensers? The villages also must have their visitors to inquire what lectures the bagpipe and the rebec reads, even to the balladry and the gamut of every municipal fiddler, for these are the countryman's Arcadias and his Monte Mayors. [23]

Next, what more national corruption, for which England hears ill [24] abroad, than household gluttony? Who shall be the rectors of our daily rioting? And what shall be done to inhibit the multitudes that frequent those houses where drunkenness is sold and harbored? Our garments also should be referred to the licensing of some more sober workmasters, to see them cut into a less-wanton garb. Who shall regulate all the mixed conversation[25] of our youth, male and female together, as is the fashion of this country? Who shall still appoint what shall be discoursed, what presumed, and no further? Lastly, who shall forbid and separate all idle resort, all evil company? These things will be, and must be; but how they shall be least hurtful, how least enticing, herein consists the grave and governing wisdom of a state.

To sequester out of the world into Atlantic and Utopian polities,[26] which never can be drawn into use, will not mend our condition; but to ordain wisely as in this world of evil, in the midst whereof God hath placed as unavoidably. Nor is it Plato's licensing of books will do this, which necessarily pulls along with it so many other kinds of licensing as will make us all both ridiculous and weary, and yet frustrate; but those unwritten or at least unconstraining laws of virtuous education, religious and civil nurture, which Plato there mentions as the bonds and ligaments of the common-

---

[22] shrewd mischievous or malicious  [23] Arcadias . . . Monte Mayors pastoral romances: Sir Philip Sidney's *Arcadia*, 1590 and Jorge de Montemayor's *Diana*, 1542  [24] hears ill is ill spoken of  [25] conversation association  [26] Atlantic . . . polities imaginary societies: Bacon's *New Atlantis*, 1627; More's *Utopia*, 1516

wealth, the pillars and the sustainers of every written statute; these they be which will bear chief sway in such matters as these, when all licensing will be easily eluded.
Impunity and remissness, for certain, are the bane of a
commonwealth; but here the great art lies, to discern in
what the law is to bid restraint and punishment, and in
what things persuasion only is to work. If every action
which is good or evil in man at ripe years were to be under
pittance,[27] and prescription, and compulsion, what were
virtue but a name, what praise could be then due to well-
doing, what gramercy[28] to be sober, just, or continent?

Many there be that complain of divine Providence for
suffering Adam to transgress. Foolish tongues! When God
gave him reason, he gave him freedom to choose, for reason
is but choosing; he had been else a mere artificial Adam,
such an Adam as he is in the motions.[29] We ourselves esteem not of that obedience, or love, or gift, which is of
force: God therefore left him free, set before him a pro-
voking object ever almost in his eyes, herein consisted his
merit, herein the right of his reward, the praise of his absti-
nence. Wherefore did he create passions within us, pleasures round about us, but that these rightly tempered are
the very ingredients of virtue? They are not skilful con-
siderers of human things, who imagine to remove sin by
removing the matter of sin; for, besides that it is a huge
heap increasing under the very act of diminishing, though
some part of it may for a time be withdrawn from some persons, it cannot from all, in such a universal thing as books
are; and when this is done, yet the sin remains entire.
Though ye take from a covetous man all his treasure, he has
yet one jewel left: ye cannot bereave him of his covetous-
ness. Banish all objects of lust, shut up all youth into the
severest discipline that can be exercised in any hermitage,
ye cannot make them chaste that came not thither so: such
great care and wisdom is required to the right managing
of this point.

[27] pittance allowance    [28] gramercy merit    [29] motions puppet
shows

Suppose we could expel sin by this means; look how much we thus expel of sin, so much we expel of virtue: for the matter of them both is the same; remove that, and ye remove them both alike. This justifies the high providence of God, who, though he command us temperance, justice, continence, yet pours out before us even to a profuseness all desirable things, and gives us minds that can wander beyond all limit and satiety. Why should we then affect a 'rigor contrary to the manner of God and of nature, by abridging or scanting those means, which books freely permitted are, both to the trial of virtue and the exercise of truth?

It would be better done to learn that the law must needs be frivolous which goes to restrain things uncertainly and yet equally working to good and to evil. And were I the chooser, a dram of well-doing should be preferred before many times as much the forcible hindrance of evil-doing. For God sure esteems the growth and completing of one virtuous person more than the restraint of ten vicious. And albeit whatever thing we hear or see, sitting, walking, travelling, or conversing, may be fitly called our book, and is of the same effect that writings are, yet grant the thing to be prohibited were only books, it appears that this order hitherto is far insufficient to the end which it intends. Do we not see, not once or oftener but weekly, that continued court-libel [30] against the Parliament and City, printed, as the wet sheets can witness, and dispersed among us, for all that licensing can do? Yet this is the prime service, a man would think, wherein this Order should give proof of itself. If it were executed, you'll say. But certain, if execution be remiss or blindfold now, and in this particular, what will it be hereafter, and in other books?

If then the Order shall not be vain and frustrate, behold a new labor, Lords and Commons: ye must repeal and proscribe all scandalous and unlicensed books already printed

---

* court-libel a royalist journal called the *Mercurius Aulicus*

and divulged;[31] after ye have drawn them up into a list, that all may know which are condemned and which not; and ordain that no foreign books be delivered out of custody, till they have been read over. This office will require the whole time of not a few overseers, and those no vulgar[32] men. There be also books which are partly useful and excellent, partly culpable and pernicious; this work will ask as many more officials to make expurgations and expunctions, that the commonwealth of learning be not damnified.[33] In fine, when the multitude of books increase upon their hands, ye must be fain to catalogue all those printers who are found frequently offending, and forbid the importation of their whole suspected typography. In a word, that this your Order may be exact and not deficient, ye must reform it perfectly according to the model of Trent and Seville,[34] which I know ye abhor to do.

Yet though ye should condescend [35] to this, which God forbid, the Order still would be but fruitless and defective to that end whereto ye meant it. If to prevent sects and schisms, who is so unread or so uncatechized in story,[36] that hath not heard of many sects refusing books as a hindrance, and preserving their doctrine unmixed for many ages, only by unwritten traditions? The Christian faith (for that was once a schism) is not unknown to have spread all over Asia, ere any Gospel or Epistle was seen in writing. If the amendment of manners be aimed at, look into Italy and Spain, whether those places be one scruple the better, the honester, the wiser, the chaster, since all the inquisitional rigor that hath been executed upon books.

Another reason, whereby to make it plain that this Order will miss the end it seeks, consider[37] by the quality which ought to be in every licenser. It cannot be denied but that he who is made judge to sit upon the birth or death of books, whether they may be wafted into this world or not,

[31] divulged published    [32] vulgar ordinary    [33] damnified damaged
[34] Seville seat of the principal court of the Spanish Inquisition
[35] condescend assent    [36] story history    [37] consider judge

had need to be a man above the common measure, both studious, learned, and judicious; there may be else no mean mistakes in the censure[38] of what is passable or not, which is also no mean injury. If he be of such worth as behooves him, there cannot be a more tedious and unpleasing journey-work,[39] a greater loss of time levied upon his head, than to be made the perpetual reader of unchosen books and pamphlets, ofttimes huge volumes. There is no book that is acceptable unless at certain seasons; but to be enjoined the reading of that at all times, and in a hand scarce legible, whereof three pages would not down at any time in the fairest print, is an imposition which I cannot believe how he that values time, and his own studies, or is but of a sensible[40] nostril, should be able to endure.

In this one thing I crave leave of the present licensers to be pardoned for so thinking: who doubtless took this office up, looking on it through their obedience to the Parliament, whose command perhaps made all things seem easy and unlaborious to them; but that this short trial hath wearied them out already, their own expressions and excuses to them who make so many journeys to solicit their license are testimony enough. Seeing therefore those who now possess the employment by all evident signs wish themselves well rid of it, and that no man of worth, none that is not a plain unthrift of his own hours, is ever likely to succeed them, except he mean to put himself to the salary of a press corrector, we may easily forsee what kind of licensers we are to expect hereafter, either ignorant, imperious, and remiss, or basely pecuniary.

This is what I had to show wherein this Order cannot conduce to that end whereof it bears the intention.

I lastly proceed from the no good it can do, to the manifest hurt it causes, in being first the greatest discouragement and affront that can be offered to learning and to learned men. It was the complaint and lamentation of prelates, upon

---

[38] censure judgment   [39] journey-work day-labor   [40] sensible sensitive

every least breath of a motion to remove pluralities[41] and distribute more equally church revenues, that then all learning would be for ever dashed and discouraged. But as for that opinion, I never found cause to think that the tenth part of learning stood or fell with the clergy: nor could I ever but hold it for a sordid and unworthy speech of any churchman who had a competency left him. If therefore ye be loath to dishearten utterly and discontent,[42] not the mercenary crew of false pretenders to learning, but the free and ingenuous sort of such as evidently were born to study and love learning for itself, not for lucre or any other end but the service of God and of truth, and perhaps that lasting fame and perpetuity of praise which God and good men have consented shall be the reward of those whose published labors advance the good of mankind: then know, that so far to distrust the judgment and the honesty of one who hath but a common repute in learning and never yet offended, as not to count him fit to print his mind without a tutor and examiner, lest he should drop a schism or something of corruption, is the greatest displeasure and indignity to a free and knowing spirit that can be put upon him.

What advantage is it to be a man, over it is to be a boy at school, if we have only escaped the ferula[43] to come under the fescue[44] of an imprimatur?—if serious and elaborate writings, as if they were no more than the theme of a grammar-lad under his pedagogue, must not be uttered without the cursory eyes of a temporizing and extemporizing licenser? He who is not trusted with his own actions, his drift not being known to be evil, and standing to the hazard of law and penalty, has no great argument to think himself reputed in the commonwealth wherein he was born for other than a fool or a foreigner. When a man writes to the world, he summons up all his reason and deliberation to assist him; he searches, meditates, is industrious, and

---

[41] pluralities the holding of two or more livings in the church concurrently by the same person  [42] discontent make discontented  [43] ferula cane  [44] fescue a small stick used as a pointer

likely consults and confers with his judicious friends; after all which done he takes himself to be informed in what he writes as well as any that writ before him; if in this, the most consummate act of his fidelity and ripeness, no years, no industry, no former proof of his abilities, can bring him to that state of maturity as not to be still mistrusted and suspected, unless he carry all his considerate diligence, all his midnight watchings, and expense of Palladian[45] oil, to the hasty view of an unleisured licenser, perhaps much his younger, perhaps far his inferior in judgment, perhaps one who never knew the labor of book-writing; and if he be not repulsed, or slighted, must appear in print like a puny[46] with his guardian, and his censor's hand on the back of his title to be his bail and surety that he is no idiot or seducer, it cannot be but a dishonor and derogation to the author, to the book, to the privilege and dignity of learning.

And what if the author shall be one so copious of fancy as to have many things well worth the adding come into his mind after licensing, while the book is yet under the press, which not seldom happens to the best and diligentest writers; and that perhaps a dozen times in one book? The printer dares not go beyond his licensed copy; so often then must the author trudge to his leave-giver, that those his new insertions may be viewed; and many a jaunt will be made, ere that licenser, for it must be the same man, can either be found or found at leisure; meanwhile either the press must stand still, which is no small damage, or the author lose his accuratest[47] thoughts, and send the book forth worse than he had made it, which to a diligent writer is the greatest melancholy and vexation that can befall.

And how can a man teach with authority, which is the life of teaching, how can he be a doctor[48] in his book as he ought to be, or else had better be silent, whenas all he teaches, all he delivers, is but under the tuition, under the correction of his patriarchal licenser, to blot or alter what

---

[45] Palladian scholarly, the oil used in a scholar's lamp  [46] puny a minor or a deficient  [47] accuratest soundest  [48] doctor teacher

precisely accords not with the hide-bound humor which he calls his judgment?—when every acute reader, upon the first sight of a pedantic[49] license, will be ready with these like words to ding[50] the book a quoit's distance from him: "I hate a pupil teacher; I endure not an instructor that comes to me under the wardship of an overseeing fist. I know nothing of the licenser, but that I have his own hand here for his arrogance; who shall warrant me his judgment?" "The State, sir," replies the stationer,[51] but has a quick return: "The State shall be my governors, but not my critics; they may be mistaken in the choice of a licenser, as easily as this licenser may be mistaken in an author; this is some common stuff." And he might add from Sir Francis Bacon,[52] that "Such authorized books are but the language of the times." For though a licenser should happen to be judicious more than ordinary, which will be a great jeopardy of the next succession, yet his very office and his commission enjoins him to let pass nothing but what is vulgarly received already.

Nay, which is more lamentable, if the work of any deceased author, though never so famous in his lifetime and even to this day, come to their hands for license to be printed or reprinted, if there be found in his book one sentence of a venturous[53] edge, uttered in the height of zeal (and who knows whether it might not be the dictate of a divine spirit), yet not suiting with every low, decrepit humor of their own, though it were Knox[54] himself, the reformer of a kingdom, that spake it, they will not pardon him their dash:[55] the sense of that great man shall to all posterity be lost for the fearfulness or the presumptuous rashness of a perfunctory licenser. And to what an author[56]

---

[49] pedantic schoolmasterly   [50] ding throw   [51] stationer publisher
[52] Bacon from An Advertisement Touching the Controversies of the Church of England, published 1640 but written 1589
[53] venturous daring   [54] Knox John (1505-1572), the Scottish reformer   [55] dash pen-stroke deleting a passage   [56] author possibly the posthumous volumes of Sir Edward Coke's Institutes, 1641, or Knox's History of the Reformation in Scotland, reissued 1644

this violence hath been lately done, and in what book of greatest consequence to be faithfully published, I could now instance, but shall forbear till a more convenient sea· son. Yet if these things be not resented seriously and timely by them who have the remedy in their power, but that such iron-moulds[57] as these shall have authority to gnaw out the choicest periods of exquisitest books, and to commit such a treacherous fraud against the orphan remainders of worthiest men after death, the more sorrow will belong to that hapless race of men, whose misfortune it is to have understanding. Henceforth let no man care to learn, or care to be more than worldly wise; for certainly in higher matters to be ignorant and slothful, to be a common steadfast[58] dunce, will be the only pleasant life and only in request.

And as it is a particular disesteem of every knowing person alive, and most injurious to the written labors and monuments of the dead, so to me it seems an undervaluing and vilifying of the whole nation. I cannot set so light by all the invention, the art, the wit, the grave and solid judg· ment which is in England, as that it can be comprehended in any twenty capacities, how good soever; much less that it should not pass except their superintendence be over it, except it be sifted and strained with their strainers, that it should be uncurrent without their manual stamp. Truth and understanding are not such wares as to be monopolised and traded in by tickets, and statutes, and standards.[59] We must not think to make a staple commodity[60] of all the knowledge in the land, to mark and license it like our broadcloth and our woolpacks. What is it but a servitude like that imposed by the Philistines, not to be allowed the sharpening of our own axes and coulters, but we must repair from all quarters to twenty licensing forges?

Had any one written and divulged erroneous things and

---

[57] iron-moulds rust spots [58] steadfast incorrigible [59] tickets . . . standards ordinary commercial operations. Tickets were evi- dences of indebtedness for goods received and statutes were securities given for such indebtedness [60] staple commodity one traded under legal monopoly

scandalous to honest life, misusing and forfeiting the esteem had of his reason among men, if after conviction this only censure were adjudged him, that he should never henceforth write but what were first examined by an appointed officer, whose hand should be annexed to pass his credit for him that now he might be safely read, it could not be apprehended less than a disgraceful punishment. Whence to include the whole nation, and those that never yet thus offended, under such a diffident[61] and suspectful prohibition, may plainly be understood what a disparagement it is. So much the more whenas debtors and delinquents may walk abroad without a keeper, but unoffensive books must not stir forth without a visible jailor in their title. Nor is it to the common people less than a reproach; for if we be so jealous[62] over them as that we dare not trust them with an English pamphlet, what do we but censure them for a giddy, vicious, and ungrounded people, in such a sick and weak estate of faith and discretion as to be able to take nothing down but through the pipe of a licenser? That this is care or love of them we cannot pretend, whenas in those popish places where the laity are most hated and despised the same strictness is used over them. Wisdom we cannot call it, because it stops but one breach of license; nor that neither, whenas those corruptions which it seeks to prevent break in faster at other doors which cannot be shut.

And in conclusion it reflects to the disrepute of our ministers also, of whose labors we should hope better, and of the proficiency which their flock reaps by them, than that after all this light of the Gospel which is, and is to be, and all this continual preaching, they should be still frequented with such an unprincipled, unedified, and laic[63] rabble, as that the whiff of every new pamphlet should stagger them out of their catechism and Christian walking. This may have much reason to discourage the ministers, when such a low conceit[64] is had of all their exhortations and the benefiting of their hearers, as that they are not thought fit to be turned

---

[61] diffident distrustful  [62] jealous suspiciously watchful  [63] laic common  [64] conceit opinion

loose to three sheets of paper without a licenser; that all the sermons, all the lectures preached, printed, vended in such numbers and such volumes as have now well-nigh made all other books unsalable, should not be armor enough against one single enchiridion,[65] without the castle St. Angelo[66] of an imprimatur.

And lest some should persuade ye, Lords and Commons, that these arguments of learned men's discouragement at this your Order are mere flourishes and not real, I could recount what I have seen and heard in other countries, where this kind of inquisition tyrannizes; when I have sat among their learned men (for that honor I had) and been counted happy to be born in such a place of philosophic freedom as they supposed England was, while themselves did nothing but bemoan the servile condition into which learning amongst them was brought; that this was it which had damped the glory of Italian wits, that nothing had been there written now these many years but flattery and fustian.[67] There it was that I found and visited the famous Galileo,[68] grown old, a prisoner to the Inquisition, for thinking in astronomy otherwise than the Franciscan and Dominican licensers thought. And though I knew that England then[69] was groaning loudest under the prelatical yoke, nevertheless I took it as a pledge of future happiness that other nations were so persuaded of her liberty.

Yet was it beyond my hope that those worthies were then breathing in her air, who should be her leaders to such a deliverance as shall never be forgotten by any revolution of time that this world hath to finish. When that was once begun, it was as little in my fear that what words of com-

---

[65] enchiridion a book small enough to be held in the hand; there is a play on words since it can mean also a dagger   [66] St. Angelo the papal fortress in Rome   [67] fustian verbiage; a coarse kind of cloth   [68] Galileo . . . prisoner Galileo was under house-arrest for publishing his *Dialogue on the Two Principal Systems of the World* after he had been ordered, some sixteen years before, to desist from teaching the Copernican astronomy   [69] then 1638, under Laud

plaint I heard among learned men of other parts uttered against the Inquisition, the same I should hear by as learned men at home uttered in time of Parliament against an order of licensing; and that so generally, that when I had disclosed myself a companion of their discontent, I might say, if without envy,[70] that he[71] whom an honest quæstorship had endeared to the Sicilians was not more by them importuned against Verres than the favorable opinion which I had among many who honor ye, and are known and respected by ye, loaded me with entreaties and persuasions that I would not despair to lay together that which just reason should bring into my mind toward the removal of an undeserved thraldom upon learning.

That this is not therefore the disburdening of a particular fancy, but the common grievance of all those who had prepared their minds and studies above the vulgar pitch, to advance truth in others and from others to entertain it, thus much may satisfy. And in their name I shall for neither friend nor foe conceal what the general murmur is: and if it come to inquisitioning again and licensing, and that we are so timorous of ourselves, and so suspicious of all men, as to fear each book, and the shaking of every leaf, before we know what the contents are; if some who but of late were little better than silenced from preaching, shall come now to silence us from reading except what they please, it cannot be guessed what is intended by some but a second tyranny over learning: and will soon put it out of controversy that bishops and presbyters are the same to us both name and thing.[72]

That these evils of prelaty which before from five or six and twenty sees were distributively charged upon[73] the

[70] without envy without being thought presumptuous  [71] he Cicero, referring to his orations against Verres for the latter's bad government in Sicily  [72] bishops . . . thing an ironical turn of the Presbyterian argument against the Episcopalians, that there is no difference of spiritual authority between bishops and presbyters (priests).  Cf. the famous last line of Milton's sonnet On the New Forcers of Conscience: "New Presbyter is but Old Priest writ large."  [73] charged upon laid as a burden on

whole people will now light wholly upon learning, is not
obscure to us: whenas now the pastor of a small unlearned
parish on the sudden shall be exalted archbishop over a
large diocese of books, and yet not remove, but keep his
other cure too, a mystical [74] pluralist. He who but of late
cried down the sole ordination of every novice bachelor of
art, and denied sole jurisdiction[75] over the simplest pa-
rishioner, shall now at home in his private chair assume
both these over worthiest and excellentest books, and ablest
authors that write them. This is not, ye Covenants and
Protestations[76] that we have made, this is not to put down
prelaty; this is but to chop[77] an episcopacy; this is but to
translate the palace metropolitan from one kind of dominion
into another; this is but an old canonical sleight[78] of com-
muting our penance. To startle thus betimes at a mere unlicensed pamphlet will, after a while, be afraid of every
conventicle,[79] and a while after will make a conventicle of
every Christian meeting.

But I am certain that a state governed by the rules of
justice and fortitude, or a church built and founded upon
the rock of faith and true knowledge, cannot be so pusil-
lanimous. While things are yet not constituted in religion,
that freedom of writing should be restrained by a discipline
imitated from the prelates and learnt by them from the
Inquisition, to shut us up all again into the breast of a
licenser, must needs give cause of doubt and discouragement to all learned and religious men; who cannot but
discern the fineness[80] of this politic drift, and who are the

---

[74] mystical covert    [75] Ordination . . . jurisdiction Again an ironical reference to the Presbyterian attack on Episcopalianism. The
two chief issues were the superior rank given to bishops mani-
fested in their sole power to ordain ministers, and the government of the church by the clergy as against the presbyterian
plan of giving lay elders equal rank with ministers    [76] Covenants
and Protestations The Covenants of 1638 and 1643 and the
Protestation of 1641 which pledged all adherents to the recovery and maintenance of true religion    [77] chop exchange
[78] canonical sleight trick of canon law    [79] conventicle a clandes-
tine or unlawful religious assembly    [80] fineness cunning

contrivers, that while bishops were to be baited down, then all the presses might be open; it was the people's birthright and privilege in time of Parliament, it was the breaking forth of light. But now, the bishops abrogated and voided out of the church, as if our reformation sought no more but to make room for others into their seats under another name, the episcopal arts begin to bud again; the cruse of truth must run no more oil; liberty of printing must be enthraled again under a prelatical commission of twenty; the privilege of the people nullified; and which is worse, the freedom of learning must groan again and to her old fetters: all this the Parliament yet sitting. Although their own late arguments and defences against the prelates might remember[81] them that this obstructing violence meets for the most part with an event utterly opposite to the end which it drives at: instead of suppressing sects and schisms, it raises them and invests them with a reputation. "The punishing of wits enhances their authority," saith the Viscount St. Albans,[82] "and a forbidden writing is thought to be a certain spark of truth that flies up in the faces of them who seek to tread it out." This Order therefore may prove a nursing mother to sects, but I shall easily show how it will be a stepdame to Truth: and first, by disenabling us to the maintenance of what is known already.

Well knows he who uses[83] to consider, that our faith and knowledge thrives by exercise, as well as our limbs and complexion.[84] Truth is compared in Scripture to a streaming fountain; if her waters flow not in a perpetual progression, they sicken into a muddy pool of conformity and tradition. A man may be a heretic in the truth; and if he believe things only because his pastor says so, or the Assembly so determines, without knowing other reason, though his belief be true, yet the very truth he holds becomes his heresy. There is not any burden that some would gladlier post off to another, than the charge and care of their religion. There

---

[81] remember remind  [82] St. Albans Francis Bacon, from the work quoted previously  [83] uses is accustomed  [84] complexion bodily constitution

be, who knows not that there be, of Protestants and professors,[85] who live and die in as arrant an implicit faith[86] as any lay papist of Loreto.[87]

A wealthy man addicted to his pleasure and to his profits finds religion to be a traffic so entangled, and of so many piddling accounts that of all mysteries[88] he cannot skill [89] to keep a stock going upon that trade. What should he do? Fain he would have the name to be religious, fain he would bear up with his neighbors in that. What does he therefore but resolves to give over toiling, and to find himself out some factor,[90] to whose care and credit he may commit the whole managing of his religious affairs, some divine of note and estimation that must be. To him he adheres, resigns the whole warehouse of his religion, with all the locks and keys, into his custody; and indeed makes the very person of that man his religion; esteems his associating with him a sufficient evidence and commendatory of his own piety. So that a man may say his religion is now no more within himself, but is become a dividual [91] movable, and goes and comes near him according as that good man frequents the house. He entertains him, gives him gifts, feasts him, lodges him; his religion comes home at night, prays, is liberally supped, and sumptuously laid to sleep; rises, is saluted, and after the malmsey, or some well-spiced brewage, and better breakfasted than He whose morning appetite would be gladly fed on green figs between Bethany and Jerusalem, his religion walks abroad at eight and leaves his kind entertainer in the shop trading all day without his religion.

Another sort there be who, when they hear that all things shall be ordered, all things regulated and settled, nothing written but what passes through the custom-house of certain

[85] professors those who profess a strict form of Christianity, Puritans  [86] implicit faith accepted on the authority of the church without inquiry  [87] Loreto in central Italy, a place of pilgrimage because of the house alleged to be the birthplace of the Virgin and to have been miraculously brought there by angels in order to save it from the Saracens  [88] mysteries trades  [89] skill know how  [90] factor agent  [91] dividual separable from himself

publicans that have the tunaging and poundaging[92] of all free-spoken truth, will straight give themselves up into your hands, make 'em and cut 'em out what religion ye please: there be delights, there be recreations and jolly pastimes that will fetch the day about from sun to sun, and rock the tedious year as in a delightful dream. What need they torture their heads with that which others have taken so strictly and so unalterably into their own purveying? These are the fruits which a dull ease and cessation of our knowledge will bring forth among the people. How goodly, and how to be wished were such an obedient unanimity as this! What a fine conformity would it starch[93] us all into! Doubtless a staunch and solid piece of framework as any January could freeze together.

Nor much better will be the consequence even among the clergy themselves. It is no new thing never heard of before for a parochial minister, who has his reward and is at his Hercules pillars[94] in a warm benefice, to be easily inclinable, if he have nothing else that may rouse up his studies, to finish his circuit[95] in an English concordance and a topic folio, the gatherings and savings of a sober graduateship, a harmony and a catena,[96] treading the constant round of certain common doctrinal heads attended with their uses, motives, marks, and means; out of which, as out of an alphabet or sol-fa,[97] by forming and transforming, joining and disjoining variously, a little bookcraft and two hours' meditation might furnish him unspeakably to the performance of more than a weekly charge of sermoning: not to reckon up the infinite helps of interlinearies,[98] brevi-

[92] publicans . . . poundaging collectors of customs duties [93] starch stiffen or make formal [94] Hercules pillars the limit of his ambition; the rocks at Gibraltar were supposed to have been placed by Hercules as the western boundary of the world [95] finish his circuit conclude his studies [96] concordance . . . catena a concordance to the Scriptures, a commonplace book with memoranda for sermons noted down while he was a student, a harmony of the Gospels, and a collection of quotations from the Fathers to serve as a commentary [97] sol-fa scale [98] interlinearies . . . gear interlinear translations, abridgments, compendiums, and similar lazy tackle

aries, synopses, and other loitering gear. But as for the multitude of sermons ready printed and piled up, on every text that is not difficult, our London trading St. Thomas in his vestry, and add to boot St. Martin and St. Hugh, have not within their hallowed limits more vendible ware of all sorts ready made:[99] so that penury he never need fear of pulpit provision, having where so plenteously to refresh his magazine. But if his rear and flanks be not impaled,[1] if his back door be not secured by the rigid licenser but that a bold book may now and then issue forth and give the assault to some of his old collections in their trenches, it will concern him then to keep waking, to stand in watch, to set good guards and sentinels about his received opinions, to walk the round and counter-round with his fellow inspectors, fearing lest any of his flock be seduced, who also then would be better instructed, better exercised and disciplined. And God send that the fear of this diligence which must then be used do not make us affect the laziness of a licensing church.

For if we be sure we are in the right, and do not hold the truth guiltily, which becomes not; if we ourselves condemn not our own weak and frivolous teaching, and the people for an untaught and irreligious, gadding rout; what can be more fair than when a man judicious, learned, and of a conscience, for aught we know, as good as theirs that taught us what we know, shall not privily from house to house, which is more dangerous, but openly by writing, publish to the world what his opinion is, what his reasons, and wherefore that which is now thought cannot be sound? Christ urged it as wherewith to justify himself that he preached in public; yet writing is more public than preaching, and more easy to refutation if need be, there being so many whose business and profession merely it is to be the champions of truth; which if they neglect, what can be imputed but their sloth or unability?

[99] **London . . . ready made** the London market is as well stocked with sermons as with any other ready-made merchandise. The reference to the churches is obscure but they were, apparently, in the commercial part of the city   [1] **impaled** protected by stakes

Thus much we are hindered and disinured [2] by this course of licensing toward the true knowledge of what we seem to know. For how much it hurts and hinders the licensers themselves in the calling of their ministry, more than any secular employment, if they will discharge that office as they ought, so that of necessity they must neglect either the one duty or the other, I insist not, because it is a particular,[3] but leave it to their own conscience how they will decide it there.

There is yet behind of what I purposed to lay open, the incredible loss and detriment that this plot of licensing puts us to; more than if some enemy at sea should stop up all our havens, and ports, and creeks, it hinders and retards the importation of our richest merchandise, truth: nay, it was first established and put in practice by antichristian malice and mystery,[4] on set purpose to extinguish, if it were possible, the light of reformation, and to settle[5] falsehood; little differing from that policy wherewith the Turk upholds his Alcoran by the prohibition of printing. 'Tis not denied, but gladly confessed, we are to send our thanks and vows to Heaven, louder than most of nations, for that great measure of truth which we enjoy, especially in those main points between us and the Pope, with his appurtenances the prelates: but he who thinks we are to pitch our tent here, and have attained the utmost prospect of reformation that the mortal glass wherein we contemplate can show us, till we come to beatific vision, that man by this very opinion declares that he is yet far short of truth.

Truth indeed came once into the world with her divine Master, and was a perfect shape most glorious to look on: but when He ascended, and His apostles after Him were laid asleep, then straight arose a wicked race of deceivers, who, as that story goes of the Egyptian Typhon[6] with his conspirators, how they dealt with the good Osiris, took the

---

[2] disinured deprived of use  [3] particular their own concern  [4] mystery craft  [5] settle establish  [6] Typhon Osiris's brother usurped his throne and murdered him and was overthrown by Isis and her son Horus after they had found Osiris's body

virgin Truth, hewed her lovely form into a thousand pieces, and scattered them to the four winds. From that time ever since, the sad friends of Truth, such as durst appear, imitating the careful [7] search that Isis made for the mangled body of Osiris, went up and down gathering up limb by limb still as they could find them. We have not yet found them all, Lords and Commons, nor ever shall do, till her Master's second coming; He shall bring together every joint and member, and shall mould them into an immortal feature[8] of loveliness and perfection. Suffer not these licensing prohibitions to stand at every place of opportunity forbidding and disturbing them that continue seeking, that continue to do our obsequies[9] to the torn body of our martyred saint.

We boast our light; but if we look not wisely on the sun itself, it smites us into darkness. Who can discern those planets that are oft combust,[10] and those stars of brightest magnitude that rise and set with the sun, until the opposite motion of their orbs bring them to such a place in the firmament where they may be seen evening or morning? The light which we have gained was given us, not to be ever staring on, but by it to discover onward things more remote from our knowledge. It is not the unfrocking of a priest, the unmitring of a bishop, and the removing him from off the Presbyterian shoulders, that will make us a happy nation; no, if other things as great in the church, and in the rule of life both economical [11] and political, be not looked into and reformed, we have looked so long upon the blaze that Zuinglius and Calvin hath beaconed up[12] to us that we are stark blind.

There be who perpetually complain of schisms and sects, and make it such a calamity that any man dissents from their maxims. 'Tis their own pride and ignorance which

---

[7] careful anxious  [8] feature creation  [9] obsequies rites  [10] combust seen close to the sun  [11] economical domestic  [12] Zuinglius . . . beaconed the reforms of Zwingli at Zürich and of Calvin at Geneva are merely signals for further reforms in church and state, not "lights to be ever staring on"

causes the disturbing, who neither will hear with meekness nor can convince, yet all must be suppressed which is not found in their syntagma.[13] They are the troublers, they are the dividers of unity, who neglect and permit not others to unite those dissevered pieces which are yet wanting to the body of Truth. To be still searching what we know not by what we know, still closing up truth to truth as we find it (for all her body is homogeneal and proportional), this is the golden rule in theology as well as in arithmetic, and makes up the best harmony in a church; not the forced and outward union of cold, and neutral, and inwardly divided minds.

Lords and Commons of England, consider what nation it is whereof ye are, and whereof ye are the governors: a nation not slow and dull, but of a quick, ingenious, and piercing spirit; acute to invent, subtle and sinewy to discourse,[14] not beneath the reach of any point the highest that human capacity can soar to. Therefore the studies of learning in her deepest sciences have been so ancient and so eminent among us that writers of good antiquity and ablest judgment have been persuaded that even the school of Pythagoras and the Persian wisdom[15] took beginning from the old philosophy of this island. And that wise and civil Roman, Julius Agricola,[16] who governed once here for Cæsar, preferred the natural wits of Britain before the labored studies of the French. Nor is it for nothing that the grave and frugal Transylvanian sends out yearly from as far as the mountainous borders of Russia and beyond the Hercynian wilderness, not their youth, but their staid men, to learn our language and our theologic arts.

Yet that which is above all this, the favor and the love of Heaven we have great argument to think in a peculiar manner propitious and propending[17] towards us. Why else was

[13] syntagma collection of doctrines   [14] discourse reason   [15] Pythagoras . . . wisdom referring to speculations that traced belief in the transmigration of souls to the Druids   [16] Agricola Roman governor of Britain, A.D. 78-85. Milton follows the biography written by Agricola's son-in-law Tacitus   [17] propending inclining

this nation chosen before any other, that out of her as out
of Sion should be proclaimed and sounded forth the first
tidings and trumpet of reformation to all Europe? And had
it not been the obstinate perverseness of our prelates against
the divine and admirable spirit of Wyclif, to suppress him
as a schismatic and innovator, perhaps neither the Bohemian Huss and Jerome, no, nor the name of Luther or of
Calvin,[18] had been ever known: the glory of reforming all
our neighbors had been completely ours. But now, as our
obdurate clergy have with violence demeaned [19] the matter,
we are become hitherto the latest and backwardest scholars
of whom God offered to have made us the teachers.

Now once again by all concurrence of signs, and by the
general instinct of holy and devout men, as they daily and
solemnly express their thoughts, God is decreeing to begin
some new and great period in his church, even to the reforming of reformation itself. What does he then but reveal
himself to his servants, and as his manner is, first to his
Englishmen; I say, as his manner is, first to us, though we
mark not the method of his counsels and are unworthy?
Behold now this vast city, a city of refuge, the mansion-
house of liberty, encompassed and surrounded with his protection; the shop of war hath not there more anvils and
hammers waking, to fashion out the plates[20] and instru-
ments of armed justice in defense of beleaguered truth,
than there be pens and heads there, sitting by their studious lamps, musing, searching, revolving new notions and
ideas wherewith to present, as with their homage and their

---

[18] **Wyclif . . . Calvin** Wyclif's attempt to reform the church in
the fourteenth century stimulated the Bohemian reformers of
the fifteenth and, Milton suggests, might have accomplished all
that the Protestant reformers did in the sixteenth, if it had not
been suppressed. There was in fact a similarity between Wyclif's
purposes and Protestantism: to make church property subject
to control by government, to diminish the authority of the
priesthood and especially of the Pope, to extend religious instruction in the vernacular and by the reading of the Bible, and
in general to reduce the importance of ceremonial    [19] **demeaned**
managed    [20] **plates** breastplates

fealty, the approaching reformation: others as fast reading, trying all things, assenting to the force of reason and convincement.

What could a man require more from a nation so pliant and so prone to seek after knowledge? What wants there to such a towardly and pregnant soil but wise and faithful laborers, to make a knowing people, a nation of prophets, of sages, and of worthies? We reckon more than five months yet to harvest; there need not be five weeks, had we but eyes to lift up, the fields are white already. Where there is much desire to learn, there of necessity will be much arguing, much writing, many opinions; for opinion in good men is but knowledge in the making. Under these fantastic terrors of sect and schism, we wrong the earnest and zealous thirst after knowledge and understanding which God hath stirred up in this city. What some lament of, we rather should rejoice at, should rather praise this pious forwardness among men, to reassume the ill-deputed care of their religion into their own hands again. A little generous prudence,[21] a little forbearance of one another, and some grain of charity might win all these diligences to join and unite in one general and brotherly search after truth, could we but forego this prelatical tradition of crowding free consciences and Christian liberties into canons and precepts of men. I doubt not, if some great and worthy stranger should come among us, wise to discern the mould and temper of a people and how to govern it, observing the high hopes and aims, the diligent alacrity of our extended thoughts and reasonings in the pursuance of truth and freedom, but that he would cry out as Pyrrhus[22] did, admiring the Roman docility and courage, "If such were my Epirots, I would not despair the greatest design that could be attempted to make a church or kingdom happy."

Yet these are the men cried out against for schismatics and sectaries; as if, while the temple of the Lord was building, some cutting, some squaring the marble, others hewing

---

[21] prudence foresight or statesmanship   [22] Pyrrhus king of Epirus whose attempt to conquer Italy was defeated in 275 B.C.

the cedars, there should be a sort of irrational men who
could not consider there must be many schisms and many
dissections made in the quarry and in the timber, ere the
house of God can be built. And when every stone is laid
artfully together, it cannot be united into a continuity, it
can but be contiguous in this world: neither can every piece
of the building be of one form; nay, rather the perfection
consists in this, that out of many moderate[23] varieties and
brotherly dissimilitudes that are not vastly disproportional
arises the goodly and the graceful symmetry that commends
the whole pile and structure.

Let us therefore be more considerate builders, more wise
in spiritual architecture, when great reformation is ex-
pected. For now the time seems come wherein Moses, the
great prophet, may sit in heaven rejoicing to see that mem-
orable and glorious wish of his fulfilled, when not only our
seventy elders, but all the Lord's people, are become prophets. No marvel then though some men, and some good men
too perhaps, but young in goodness, as Joshua then was,
envy[24] them. They fret, and out of their own weakness are
in agony, lest these divisions and subdivisions will undo us.
The adversary[25] again applauds, and waits the hour: when
they have branched themselves out, saith he, small enough
into parties and partitions, then will be our time. Fool! He
sees not the firm root out of which we all grow, though into
branches; nor will beware until he see our small divided
maniples[26] cutting through at every angle of his ill-united
and unwieldy brigade. And that we are to hope better of
all these supposed sects and schisms, and that we shall not
need that solicitude, honest perhaps though over-timorous,
of them that vex in this behalf, but shall laugh in the end
at those malicious applauders of our differences, I have
these reasons to persuade me.

First, when a city shall be as it were besieged and

---

[23] moderate not extreme [24] envy disapprove [25] adversary the
church of Rome [26] maniples companies; the divisions of Protestantism compared with the "unwieldy" unity of Catholicism

blocked about, her navigable river infested, inroads and incursions round, defiance and battle oft rumored to be marching up even to her walls and suburb trenches; that then the people, or the greater part, more than at other times, wholly taken up with the study of highest and most important matters to be reformed, should be disputing, reasoning, reading, inventing, discoursing, even to a rarity and admiration,[27] things not before discoursed or written of, argues first a singular good will, contentedness, and confidence in your prudent foresight and safe government, Lords and Commons; and from thence derives itself[28] to a gallant bravery and well grounded contempt of their enemies, as if there were no small number of as great spirits among us, as his was, who, when Rome was nigh besieged by Hannibal, being in the city, bought that piece of ground at no cheap rate whereon Hannibal himself encamped his own regiment.

Next, it is a lively and cheerful presage of our happy success and victory. For as in a body, when the blood is fresh, the spirits pure and vigorous, not only to vital but to rational faculties, and those in the acutest and the pertest[29] operations of wit and subtlety, it argues in what good plight and constitution the body is; so when the cheerfulness of the people is so sprightly up, as that it has not only wherewith to guard well its own freedom and safety but to spare, and to bestow upon the solidest and sublimest points of controversy and new invention, it betokens us not degenerated, nor drooping to a fatal decay, but casting off the old and wrinkled skin of corruption to outlive these pangs and wax young again, entering the glorious ways of truth and prosperous virtue destined to become great and honorable in these latter ages.

Methinks I see in my mind a noble and puissant nation rousing herself like a strong man after sleep, and shaking her invincible locks:[30] methinks I see her as an eagle mew-

---

[27] even . . . admiration to a rare and admirable degree    [28] derives itself proceeds    [29] pertest liveliest    [30] locks cf. the story of Samson, *Judges* xvi, 6-20

ing[81] her mighty youth, and kindling her undazzled eyes at the full midday beam; purging and unscaling her long-abused sight at the fountain itself of heavenly radiance; while the whole noise of timorous and flocking birds,[82] with those also that love the twilight, flutter about, amazed at what she means, and in their envious gabble would prognosticate a year of sects and schisms.

What should ye do then, should ye suppress all this flowery crop of knowledge and new light sprung up and yet springing daily in this city, should ye set an oligarchy of twenty engrossers[83] over it, to bring a famine upon our minds again, when we shall know nothing but what is measured to us by their bushel? Believe it, Lords and Commons, they who counsel ye to such a suppressing do as good as bid ye suppress yourselves; and I will soon show how. If it be desired to know the immediate cause of all this free writing and free speaking, there cannot be assigned a truer than your own mild, and free, and humane government; it is the liberty, Lords and Commons, which your own valorous and happy counsels have purchased us, liberty which is the nurse of all great wits; this is that which hath rarefied and enlightened our spirits like the influence of heaven; this is that which hath enfranchised, enlarged, and lifted up our apprehensions degrees above themselves. Ye cannot make us now less capable, less knowing, less eagerly pursuing of the truth, unless ye first make yourselves, that made us so, less the lovers, less the founders of our true liberty. We can grow ignorant again, brutish, formal, and slavish, as ye found us; but you then must first become that which ye cannot be, oppressive, arbitrary, and tyrannous, as they were from whom ye have freed us. That our hearts are now more capacious, our thoughts more erected to the search and expectation of greatest and exactest[84] things, is the issue of your own virtue propagated in us; ye cannot suppress that unless ye reinforce[35] an

---

[81] mewing moulting; probably in the sense of renewing  [82] noise . . . birds concert of birds that flock because they are timorous  [83] engrossers monopolists  [84] exactest most perfect  [35] reinforce put in force again

abrogated and merciless law, that fathers may despatch at will their own children.[36] And who shall then stick closest to ye and excite others? Not he who takes up arms for coat and conduct, and his four nobles of Danegelt.[37] Although I dispraise not the defence of just immunities, yet love my peace better, if that were all. Give me the liberty to know, to utter, and to argue freely according to conscience, above all liberties.

What would be best advised then, if it be found so hurtful and so unequal [38] to suppress opinions for the newness or the unsuitableness to a customary acceptance, will not be my task to say; I only shall repeat what I have learned from one of your own honorable number, a right noble and pious lord, who, had he not sacrificed his life and fortunes to the church and commonwealth, we had not now missed and bewailed a worthy and undoubted patron of this argument. Ye know him I am sure; yet I for honor's sake, and may it be eternal to him, shall name him, the Lord Brooke.[39] He, writing of episcopacy, and by the way treating of sects and schisms, left ye his vote,[40] or rather now the last words of his dying charge, which I know will ever be of dear and honored regard with ye, so full of meekness and breathing

---

[36] fathers . . . children in primitive Roman Law [37] Not . . . Danegelt not one who regards illegal taxation as the principal grievance against the King. Coat and conduct money was a tax levied for outfitting and assembling troops. Danegelt means shipmoney; the ancient levy to protect the country against invasion was cited as a precedent by the Crown in the suit against John Hampden (1637-38). The King's effort to collect both these taxes without parliamentary approval had been an important issue before the Civil War. Four nobles ( £ 1.6s.8d.) seems to be mentioned to enforce the trifling importance of this issue compared with free speech; the sum at stake in Hampden's case was only 20s. [38] unequal unjust [39] Lord Brooke Robert Greville, an honored parliamentary general who was killed in action in 1643. The book mentioned was entitled, *A Discourse Opening the Nature of that Episcopacy which Is Exercised in England,* 1641 [40] vote earnest desire

charity, that next to His last testament who bequeathed love
and peace to His disciples, I cannot call to mind where I
have read or heard words more mild and peaceful. He there
exhorts us to hear with patience and humility those, however they be miscalled, that desire to live purely, in such a
use of God's ordinances as the best guidance of their conscience gives them, and to tolerate them, though in some
disconformity to ourselves. The book itself will tell us more
at large, being published to the world and dedicated to the
Parliament by him who, both for his life and for his death,
deserves that what advice he left be not laid by without
perusal.

And now the time in special is,[41] by privilege to write
and speak what may help to the further discussing of matters in agitation. The temple of Janus with his two contro-
versal faces might now not unsignificantly be set open.[42]
And though all the winds of doctrine were let loose to play
upon the earth, so Truth be in the field, we do injuriously
by licensing and prohibiting to misdoubt her strength. Let
her and Falsehood grapple; who ever knew Truth put to
the worse in a free and open encounter? Her confuting is
the best and surest suppressing. He who hears what pray-
ing there is for light and clearer knowledge to be sent down
among us, would think of other matters to be constituted
beyond the discipline of Geneva,[43] framed and fabriced[44]
already to our hands.

Yet when the new light which we beg for shines in upon
us, there be who envy and oppose, if it come not first in at
their casements. What a collusion is this, whenas we are
exhorted by the wise man to use diligence, "to seek for
wisdom as for hidden treasures" early and late, that another

---

[41] **And . . . is** now the time is especially fitting　　[42] **temple . . .
open** the present is a time of battle between Truth and Falsehood. The Temple of Janus in Rome had two doors facing in
opposite directions which were opened in time of war　　[43] **discipline . . . Geneva** the reforms already achieved by Calvin,
which satisfy the Presbyterians　　[44] **fabriced** constructed

order shall enjoin us to know nothing but by statute! When a man hath been laboring the hardest labor in the deep mines of knowledge, hath furnished out his findings in all their equipage, drawn forth his reasons as it were a battle[45] ranged, scattered and defeated all objections in his way, calls out his adversary into the plain, offers him the advantage of wind and sun, if he please, only that he may try the matter by dint of argument; for his opponents then to skulk, to lay ambushments, to keep a narrow bridge of licensing where the challenger should pass, though it be valor enough in soldiership, is but weakness and cowardice in the wars of Truth. For who knows not that Truth is strong next to the Almighty? She needs no policies, nor stratagems, nor licensings to make her victorious; those are the shifts and the defences that error uses against her power: give her but room, and do not bind her when she sleeps, for then she speaks not true, as the old Proteus[46] did, who spake oracles only when he was caught and bound, but then rather she turns herself into all shapes except her own, and perhaps tunes her voice according to the time, as Micaiah did before Ahab, until she be adjured into her own likeness.

Yet is it not impossible that she may have more shapes than one. What else is all that rank of things indifferent,[47] wherein Truth may be on this side or on the other, without being unlike herself? What but a vain shadow else is the abolition of "those ordinances, that hand-writing nailed to the cross," what great purchase[48] is this Christian liberty which Paul so often boasts of? His doctrine is, that he who eats or eats not, regards a day or regards it not, may do either to the Lord. How many other things might be tolerated in peace and left to conscience, had we but charity, and were it not the chief stronghold of our hypocrisy to be

[45] battle army  [46] Proteus a prophetic old man of the sea who could assume many shapes to escape prophesying, unless he were caught and bound  [47] things indifferent non-essential observances that may equally be done or omitted  [48] purchase advantage

ever judging one another! I fear yet this iron yoke of outward conformity hath left a slavish print upon our necks; the ghost of a linen decency[49] yet haunts us. We stumble and are impatient at the least dividing of one visible congregation from another, though it be not in fundamentals; and through our forwardness to suppress, and our backwardness to recover any enthralled piece of truth out of the grip of custom, we care not to keep[50] truth separated from truth, which is the fiercest rent and disunion of all. We do not see that while we still affect by all means a rigid external formality, we may as soon fall again into a gross conforming stupidity, a stark and dead congealment of "wood and hay and stubble" forced and frozen together, which is more to the sudden degenerating of a church than many subdichotomies[51] of petty schisms.

Not that I can think well of every light separation, or that all in a church is to be expected "gold and silver and precious stones": it is not possible for man to sever the wheat from the tares, the good fish from the other fry; that must be the angels' ministry at the end of mortal things. Yet if all cannot be of one mind—as who looks they should be?—this doubtless is more wholesome, more prudent, and more Christian: that many be tolerated rather than all compelled. I mean not tolerated popery and open superstition, which as it extirpates all religions and civil supremacies, so itself should be extirpate, provided first that all charitable and compassionate means be used to win and regain the weak and the misled: that also which is impious or evil absolutely, either against faith or manners,[52] no law can possibly permit that intends not to unlaw itself: but those neighboring differences, or rather indifferences, are what I speak of, whether in some point of doctrine or of discipline, which though they may be many, yet need not interrupt the unity of spirit, if we could but find among us the bond of peace.

[49] linen decency religious formalism, typified by vestments  [50] care not . . . keep are indifferent to keeping  [51] subdichotomies minor divisions  [52] manners morals

In the meanwhile, if any one would write, and bring his helpful hand to the slow-moving reformation which we labor under, if truth have spoken to him before others, or but seemed at least to speak, who hath so bejesuited us that we should trouble that man with asking license to do so worthy a deed?—and not consider this, that if it come to prohibiting, there is not aught more likely to be prohibited than truth itself: whose first appearance to our eyes, bleared and dimmed with prejudice and custom, is more unsightly and unplausible than many errors; even as the person is of many a great man slight and contemptible to see to.[53] And what do they tell us vainly of new opinions, when this very opinion of theirs, that none must be heard but whom they like, is the worst and newest opinion of all others; and is the chief cause why sects and schisms do so much abound, and true knowledge is kept at distance from us; besides yet a greater danger which is in it. For when God shakes a kingdom with strong and healthful commotions to a general reforming, 'tis not untrue that many sectaries and false teachers are then busiest in seducing; but yet more true it is that God then raises to his own work men of rare abilities and more than common industry, not only to look back and revise what hath been taught heretofore, but to gain further and go on some new enlightened steps in the discovery of truth.

For such is the order of God's enlightening his church, to dispense and deal out by degrees his beam, so as our earthly eyes may best sustain it. Neither is God appointed and confined, where and out of what place these his chosen shall be first heard to speak; for he sees not as man sees, chooses not as a man chooses, lest we should devote ourselves again to set places, and assemblies, and outward callings of men; planting our faith one while in the old Convocation house, and another while in the Chapel at

[53] to see to to look at

Westminster;[54] when all the faith and religion that shall
be there canonized is not sufficient, without plain convincement and the charity of patient instruction, to supple the
least bruise of conscience, to edify the meanest Christian
who desires to walk in the Spirit, and not in the letter of
human trust, for all the number of voices that can be there
made; no, though Harry VII himself there, with all his liege
tombs[55] about him, should lend them voices from the dead
to swell their number.

And if the men be erroneous who appear to be the leading schismatics, what withholds us but our sloth, our self-
will, and distrust in the right cause, that we do not give
them gentle meetings and gentle dismissions, that we debate not and examine the matter thoroughly with liberal
and frequent audience; if not for their sakes, yet for our
own?—seeing no man who hath tasted learning but will
confess the many ways of profiting by those who, not contented with stale receipts, are able to manage[56] and set
forth new positions to the world. And were they but as the
dust and cinders of our feet, so long as in that notion[57] they
may yet serve to polish and brighten the armory of Truth,
even for that respect they were not utterly to be cast away.
But if they be of those whom God hath fitted for the special
use of these times with eminent and ample gifts, and those
perhaps neither among the priests nor among the pharisees,[58] and we in the haste of a precipitant zeal shall make
no distinction, but resolve to stop their mouths, because
we fear they come with new and dangerous opinions, as we
commonly forejudge them ere we understand them; no less

[54] Convocation . . . Westminster Convocation was the national
assemblage of the clergy of the Anglican Church, which had
met in the Chapter-house at Westminster. The Presbyterian Assembly of Divines, to which Parliament had transferred the
powers of Convocation, was meeting, when Milton wrote, in
Henry VII's Chapel    [55] tombs the Chapel was the burial place
of the kings and queens who were Henry's descendants
[56] manage take up a subject    [57] notion character    [58] priests . . .
pharisees having no official claim to be heard

than woe to us, while thinking thus to defend the Gospel, we are found the persecutors.

There have been not a few since the beginning[59] of this Parliament, both of the presbytery and others, who by their unlicensed books to the contempt of an imprimatur first broke that triple ice clung[60] about our hearts, and taught the people to see day: I hope that none of those were the persuaders to renew upon us this bondage, which they themselves have wrought so much good by contemning. But if neither the check that Moses gave to young Joshua, nor the countermand which our Saviour gave to young John, who was so ready to prohibit those whom he thought unlicensed, be not enough to admonish our elders[61] how unacceptable to God their testy mood of prohibiting is; if neither their own remembrance what evil hath abounded in the church by this let[62] of licensing, and what good they themselves have begun by transgressing it, be not enough but that they will persuade and execute the most Dominican[63] part of the Inquisition over us, and are already with one foot in the stirrup so active at suppressing, it would be no unequal distribution in the first place to suppress the suppressors themselves, whom the change of their condition hath puffed up more than their late experience of harder times hath made wise.

And as for regulating the press, let no man think to have the honor of advising ye better than yourselves have done in that order published next before this,[64] "that no book be printed, unless the printer's and the author's name, or at least the printer's, be registered." Those which otherwise come forth, if they be found mischievous and libellous, the fire and the executioner will be the timeliest and the most effectual remedy that man's prevention can use. For this authentic Spanish policy of licensing books, if I have said aught, will prove the most unlicensed book itself within a short while; and was the immediate image of a Star Cham-

---

[59] beginning November, 1640   [60] clung congealed   [61] elders the Presbyterians   [62] let obstruction   [63] Dominican the inquisitors were largely members of the Dominican Order   [64] order . . . this adopted by the Commons, January 29, 1642

ber decree[65] to that purpose made in those very times when that Court did the rest of those her pious works, for which she is now fallen from the stars with Lucifer. Whereby ye may guess what kind of state prudence,[66] what love of the people, what care of religion or good manners there was at the contriving, although with singular hypocrisy it pretended to bind books to their good behavior. And how it got the upper hand of your precedent order so well constituted before, if we may believe those men whose profession gives them cause to inquire most, it may be doubted [67] there was in it the fraud of some old patentees and monopolisers in the trade of bookselling; who, under pretence of the poor in their Company not to be defrauded, and the just retaining of each man his several copy,[68] which God forbid should be gainsaid, brought divers glossing colors[69] to the House, which were indeed but colors, and serving to no end except it be to exercise a superiority over their neighbors (men who do not therefore labor in an honest profession to which learning is indebted) that they should be made other men's vassals. Another end is thought was aimed at by some of them in procuring by petition this Order, that having power in their hands, malignant[70] books might the easier scape abroad, as the event shows.

But of these sophisms and elenchs of merchandise[71] I skill not. This I know, that errors in a good government and in a bad are equally almost incident; for what magistrate may not be misinformed, and much the sooner, if liberty of printing be reduced into the power of a few? But to redress willingly and speedily what hath been erred, and in highest authority to esteem a plain advertisement[72] more than others have done a sumptuous bribe, is a virtue, honored Lords and Commons, answerable to your highest actions, and whereof none can participate but greatest and wisest men.

---

[65] decree a licensing order issued in 1637. Star Chamber was abolished in 1641 [66] state prudence statesmanship [67] doubted suspected [68] copy copyright [69] glossing colors misrepresentations [70] malignant royalist [71] sophisms . . . merchandise commercial trickery [72] advertisement statement or notification

# OF EDUCATION

❧

*Master Hartlib,*

I am long since persuaded that to say or do aught worth memory and imitation, no purpose or respect should sooner move us than simply the love of God and of mankind. Nevertheless to write now the reforming of education, though it be one of the greatest and noblest designs that can be thought on, and for the want whereof this nation perishes, I had not[2] yet at this time been induced, but by your earnest entreaties and serious conjurements; as having my mind for the present half diverted in the pursuance of some other assertions,[3] the knowledge and the use of which cannot but be a great furtherance both to the enlargement[4] of truth, and honest living with much more peace.[5] Nor should the laws of any private friendship have

---

[1] Samuel Hartlib was a London merchant who had been born in Prussia of a Polish father and an English mother. He gave most of his time, and spent most of his money, in furthering a variety of public-spirited causes, including a plan for uniting all the Protestant churches, many projects for the improvement of agriculture, and ideas for reforming education. He was instrumental in publishing Comenius's books on education in England and in bringing Comenius himself to that country. Apparently he made a practice of asking his friends for plans of new educational institutions, for he made that request also of Sir William Petty, one of the founders of the Royal Society. Hartlib carried on an extensive correspondence with scholars abroad and had a vast circle of acquaintances in England  [2] had not should not have  [3] assertions arguments; presumably his pamphlets on divorce and the *Areopagitica*  [4] enlargement diffusion  [5] peace domestic peace; the object of Milton's writing on divorce

prevailed with me to divide thus or transpose my former thoughts, but that I see those aims, those actions, which have won you with me the esteem of a person sent hither by some good providence from a far country to be the occasion and the incitement of great good to this island.

And, as I hear, you have obtained the same repute with men of most approved wisdom and some of highest authority among us; not to mention the learned correspondence which you hold in foreign parts and the extraordinary pains and diligence which you have used in this matter, both here and beyond the seas; either by the definite will of God so ruling or the peculiar sway of nature, which also is God's working. Neither can I think that, so reputed and so valued as you are, you would, to the forfeit of your own discerning ability, impose upon me an unfit and over-ponderous argument,[6] but that[7] the satisfaction which you profess to have received from those incidental discourses which we have wandered into hath pressed and almost constrained you into a persuasion,[8] that what you require from me in this point, I neither ought nor can in conscience defer beyond this time both of so much need at once, and so much opportunity to try what God hath determined.

I will not resist therefore whatever it is, either of divine or human obligement, that you lay upon me; but will forthwith set down in writing, as you request me, that voluntary idea,[9] which hath long in silence presented itself to me, of a better education, in extent and comprehension far more large, and yet of time far shorter and of attainment far more certain, than hath been yet in practice. Brief I shall endeavor to be; for that which I have to say, assuredly this nation hath extreme need should be done sooner than spoken. To tell you therefore what I have benefited herein among old renowned authors, I shall spare; and to search

---

[6] over-ponderous argument too difficult subject  [7] but that unless  [8] persuasion conviction  [9] voluntary idea plan that has spontaneously presented itself

what many modern Januas and Didactics,[10] more than ever
I shall read, have projected, my inclination leads me not.
But if you can accept of these few observations which have
flowered off, and are as it were the burnishing[11] of many
studious and contemplative years altogether spent in the
search of religious and civil knowledge, and such as pleased
you so well in the relating, I here give you them to dis-
pose of.

The end then of learning is to repair the ruins of our first
parents[12] by regaining to know God aright and out of that
knowledge to love Him, to imitate Him, to be like Him,
as we may the nearest[13] by possessing our souls of true
virtue, which being united to the heavenly grace of faith
makes up the highest perfection. But because our understanding cannot in this body found itself but on sensible[14]
things, nor arrive so clearly to the knowledge of God and
things invisible as by orderly conning over[15] the visible and
inferior creature,[16] the same method is necessarily to be
followed in all discreet teaching. And seeing every nation
affords not experience and tradition enough for all kind
of learning, therefore we are chiefly taught the languages of
those people who have at any time been most industrious
after wisdom; so that language is but the instrument con-
veying to us things useful to be known. And though a lin-

---

[10] Januas and Didactics a reference to two books by the famous
Bohemian educational reformer, John Amos Comenius (1592-
1670). Comenius visited England in 1641, by Hartlib's influence
presented his ideas to Parliament, and was prevented by the
Civil War from opening an experimental college. His educational
ideas, despite the slighting tone of Milton's reference, were similar to Milton's: that languages should be taught by use rather
than for their own sake and that other subjects should be graded
in difficulty beginning with the more concrete   [11] flowered . . .
burnishing arisen as products of   [12] ruins . . . parents caused
by the fall of man   [13] nearest most nearly   [14] sensible percep-
tible by the senses   [15] conning over studying   [16] creature creation

guist should pride himself to have all the tongues that Babel
cleft the world into, yet, if he have not studied the solid
things in them as well as the words and lexicons, he were
nothing so much to be esteemed a learned man as any yeo-
man or tradesman competently wise in his mother dialect
only.

Hence appear the many mistakes which have made learning generally so unpleasing and so unsuccessful; first, we
do amiss to spend seven or eight years merely in scraping
together so much miserable Latin and Greek as might be
learned otherwise easily and delightfully in one year. And
that which casts our proficiency therein so much behind is
our time lost, partly in too oft idle vacancies[17] given both
to schools and universities, partly in a preposterous exaction,[18] forcing the empty wits of children to compose
themes, verses, and orations, which are the acts of ripest
judgment and the final work of a head filled by long reading and observing with elegant[19] maxims and copious invention. These are not matters to be wrung from poor
striplings, like blood out of the nose or the plucking of
untimely fruit: besides the ill habit which they get of
wretched barbarizing against the Latin and Greek idiom
with their untutored Anglicisms,[20] odious to be read, yet
not to be avoided without a well-continued and judicious
conversing among[21] pure authors digested, which they
scarce taste. Whereas, if after some preparatory grounds
of speech by their certain forms got into memory they were
led to the praxis[22] thereof in some chosen short book lessoned [23] thoroughly to them, they might then forthwith
proceed to learn the substance of good things and arts in
due order, which would bring the whole language quickly
into their power. This I take to be the most rational and
most profitable way of learning languages, and whereby we

---

[17] **vacancies** vacations   [18] **preposterous** exaction requirement that
**inverts** the natural order   [19] **elegant** apt   [20] **Anglicisms** English
**idioms** taken over literally into Latin or Greek   [21] **conversing**
**among** familiarity with   [22] **praxis** use or practice   [23] **lessoned**
**taught**

may best hope to give account to God of our youth spent herein.

And for the usual method of teaching arts, I deem it to be an old error of universities not yet well recovered from the scholastic grossness of barbarous ages, that instead of beginning with arts most easy (and those be such as are most obvious to the sense), they present their young un-matriculated [24] novices, at first coming, with the most intel-lective[25] abstractions of logic and metaphysics: so that they having but newly left those grammatic flats and shallows where they stuck unreasonably to learn a few words with lamentable construction, and now on the sudden trans-ported under another climate to be tossed and turmoiled with their unballasted wits in fathomless and unquiet deeps of controversy, do for the most part grow into hatred and contempt of learning, mocked and deluded all this while with ragged [26] notions and babblements, while they ex-pected worthy and delightful knowledge, till povorty or youthful years[27] call them importunately their several ways and hasten them, with the sway of friends, either to an am-bitious and mercenary or ignorantly zealous divinity; some allured to the trade of law, grounding their purposes not on the prudent[28] and heavenly contemplation of justice and equity, which was never taught them, but on the promising and pleasing thoughts of litigious terms, fat contentions, and flowing fees; others betake them to state affairs with souls so unprincipled in virtue and true generous breeding that flattery and court shifts and tyrannous aphorisms appear to them the highest points of wisdom, instilling their barren hearts with a conscientious slavery[29]—if, as I rather think, it be not feigned. Others, lastly, of a more delicious and airy[30] spirit, retire themselves (knowing no better) to the

[24] unmatriculated immature  [25] intellective to be grasped by intellect only  [26] ragged literally, shaggy; expressing Milton's opinion of scholastic philosophy  [27] youthful years restlessness of youth  [28] prudent wise  [29] conscientious slavery unreasoning devotion to routine duties  [30] delicious and airy dainty and lively

enjoyments of ease and luxury, living out their days in feast
and jollity; which indeed is the wisest and the safest course
of all these, unless they were with more integrity undertaken. And these are the errors, these are the fruits of mis-
spending our prime youth at the schools and universities
as we do, either in learning mere words or such things
chiefly as were better unlearned.

I shall detain you now no longer in the demonstration
of what we should not do, but straight conduct ye to a
hillside, where I will point ye out the right path of a virtuous and noble education; laborious indeed at the first
ascent, but else so smooth, so green, so full of goodly prospect and melodious sounds on every side, that the harp of
Orpheus was not more charming. I doubt not but ye shall
have more ado to drive our dullest and laziest youth, our
stocks and stubs, from the infinite desire of such a happy
nurture than we have now to hale and drag our choicest
and hopefullest wits to that asinine feast of sow-thistles and
brambles, which is commonly set before them as all the
food and entertainment of their tenderest and most docible[31] age. I call therefore a complete and generous education that which fits a man to perform justly, skilfully, and
magnanimously all the offices, both private and public, of
peace and war. And how all this may be done between
twelve and one-and-twenty, less time than is now bestowed
in pure trifling at grammar and sophistry, is to be thus
ordered.

First, to find out a spacious house and ground about it
fit for an academy and big enough to lodge a hundred and
fifty persons, whereof twenty or thereabout may be attendants, all under the government of one, who shall be thought
of desert sufficient and ability either to do all or wisely to
direct and oversee it done. This place should be at once
both school and university, not needing a remove to any
other house of scholarship, except it be some peculiar[32]
college of law or physic,[33] where they mean to be prac-
titioners; but as for those general studies which take up all

---

[a] docible formative   [a] peculiar special   [a] physic medicine

our time from Lily[34] to the commencing,[35] as they term it, master of art, it should be absolute.[36] After this pattern as many edifices may be converted to this use as shall be needful in every city throughout this land, which would tend much to the increase of learning and civility[37] everywhere. This number, less or more thus collected, to the convenience of a foot company or interchangeably two troops of cavalry, should divide their day's work into three parts as it lies orderly: their studies, their exercise, and their diet.

For their studies: first, they should begin with the chief and necessary rules of some good grammar, either that now used or any better: and while this is doing, their speech is to be fashioned to a distinct and clear pronunciation, as near as may be to the Italian, especially in the vowels. For we Englishmen, being far northerly, do not open our mouths in the cold air wide enough to grace a southern tongue, but are observed by all other nations to speak exceeding close and inward; so that to smatter[38] Latin with an English mouth is as ill a hearing as law-French.[39] Next, to make them expert in the usefullest points of grammar, and withal to season them and win them early to the love of virtue and true labor, ere any flattering seducement or vain principle seize them wandering, some easy and delightful book of education[40] would be read to them, whereof the Greeks have store, as Cebes, Plutarch, and other Socratic discourses. But in Latin we have none of classic authority extant, except the two or three first books of Quintilian and some select pieces elsewhere.

But here the main skill and groundwork will be to temper[41] them such lectures and explanations, upon every opportunity, as may lead and draw them in willing obedience,

[34] **Lily** William Lily's grammar was commonly the beginning book in Latin  [35] **commencing** taking the degree  [36] **absolute** complete  [37] **civility** cultivation  [38] **smatter** chatter  [39] **law-French** the French used in the English courts had got a pronunciation of its own  [40] **education** a moral work extolling knowledge and virtue, such as the Socratic dialogues in Plutarch's *Moralia*  [41] **temper** devise

inflamed with the study[42] of learning and the admiration of virtue, stirred up with high hopes of living to be brave men and worthy patriots, dear to God and famous to all ages; that they may despise and scorn all their childish and ill-taught qualities, to delight in manly and liberal exercises: which he who hath the art and proper eloquence to catch them with, what with mild and effectual [43] persuasions, and what with the intimation of some fear, if need be, but chiefly by his own example, might in a short space gain them to an incredible diligence and courage, infusing into their young breasts such an ingenuous and noble ardor as would not fail to make many of them renowned and matchless men. At the same time, some other hour of the day, might be taught them the rules of arithmetic; and soon after the elements of geometry, even playing,[44] as the old manner was. After evening repast, till bedtime, their thoughts will be best taken up in the easy grounds of religion and the story of Scripture.

The next step would be to the authors [of] agriculture, Cato, Varro, and Columella; for the matter is most easy, and if the language be difficult, so much the better: it is not a difficulty above their years. And here will be an occasion of inciting and enabling them hereafter to improve the tillage of their country, to recover the bad soil and to remedy the waste that is made of good; for this was one of Hercules' praises. Ere half these authors be read (which will soon be with plying hard and daily) they cannot choose but be masters of any ordinary prose. So that it will be then seasonable for them to learn in any modern author the use of the globes and all the maps; first with the old names and then with the new. Or they might be then capable to read any compendious method [45] of natural philosophy.

And at the same time might be entering into the Greek tongue, after the same manner as was before prescribed in the Latin; whereby the difficulties of grammar being soon

[a] study desire [b] effectual earnest [c] playing by the use of games [d] method system

overcome, all the historical physiology[46] of Aristotle and Theophrastus are open before them and, as I may say, under contribution.[47] The like access will be to Vitruvius, to Seneca's natural questions, to Mela, Celsus, Pliny, or Solinus.[48] And having thus passed the principles of arithmetic, geometry, astronomy, and geography, with a general compact of physics,[49] they may descend in mathematics to the instrumental science of trigonometry, and from thence to fortification, architecture, enginery,[50] or navigation. And in natural philosophy they may proceed leisurely from the history of meteors, minerals, plants, and living creatures, as far as anatomy.

Then also in course[51] might be read to them, out of some not tedious writer, the institution of physic,[52] that they may know the tempers, the humors,[53] the seasons,[54] and how to manage a crudity;[55] which he who can wisely and timely do is not only a great physician to himself and to his friends, but also may at some time or other save an army by this frugal and expenseless means only, and not let the healthy and stout bodies of young men rot away under him for want of this discipline; which is a great pity and no less a shame to the commander. To set forward all these proceedings[56] in nature and mathematics, what hinders but that they may procure, as oft as shall be needful, the helpful experiences of hunters, fowlers, fishermen, shepherds, gardeners, apothecaries; and in the other sciences, architects, engineers, mariners, anatomists; who doubtless would be ready, some for reward and some to favor such a hope-

[46] historical physiology natural history [47] under contribution at their command to be used as needed [48] Vitruvius . . . Solinus Vitruvius wrote on architecture; the other writers mentioned chiefly on geography or natural history [49] compact of physics outline of natural science [50] enginery military engineering [51] in course in due course [52] institution . . . physic principles of medicine [53] tempers . . . humors the four fluids of the body —blood, phlegm, yellow and black bile—were supposed by their proportions to determine a person's temperament [54] seasons their influence on health [55] crudity indigestion [56] set . . . proceedings to promote this advance

ful seminary? And this will give them such a real tincture of natural knowledge as they shall never forget, but daily augment with delight. Then also those poets which are now counted most hard will be both facile[57] and pleasant, Orpheus, Hesiod, Theocritus, Aratus, Nicander, Oppian, Dionysius; and in Latin, Lucretius, Manilius, and the rural part of Virgil.

By this time[58] years and good general precepts will have furnished them more distinctly with that act of reason which in ethics is called proairesis,[59] that they may with some judgment contemplate upon moral good and evil. Then will be required a special reinforcement of constant and sound indoctrinating to set them right and firm, instructing them more amply in the knowledge of virtue and the hatred of vice; while their young and pliant affections are led through all the moral works of Plato, Xenophon, Cicero, Plutarch, Laertius, and those Locrian remnants; but still to be reduced in their nightward studies, wherewith they close the day's work, under the determinate sentence[60] of David or Solomon, or the evangels[61] and apostolic Scriptures. Being perfect in the knowledge of personal duty, they may then begin the study of economics.[62] And either now or before this they may have easily learned, at any odd hour, the Italian tongue. And soon after, but with wariness and good antidote,[63] it would be wholesome enough to let them taste some choice comedies, Greek, Latin, or Italian; those tragedies, also, that treat of household matters, as *Trachiniæ, Alcestis,*[64] and the like.

The next remove must be to the study of politics, to know the beginning, end, and reasons of political societies; that they may not, in a dangerous fit of the commonwealth, be such poor, shaken, uncertain reeds, of such a tottering conscience, as many of our great counsellors have lately shown

[57] facile because the poets mentioned write of nature or of rural and pastoral subjects   [58] time probably at about sixteen years of age   [59] proairesis deliberate choice   [60] reduced . . . sentence conformed to the final judgment   [61] evangels Gospels   [62] economics management of a household or estate   [63] antidote to offset any bad influence of the comedians   [64] Trachiniae . . . Alcestis The *Trachiniae* of Sophocles and the *Alcestis* of Euripides

themselves, but steadfast pillars of the state. After this they are to dive into the grounds of law and legal justice; delivered first and with best warrant[65] by Moses; and as far as human prudence can be trusted, in those extolled remains of Grecian lawgivers,[66] Lycurgus, Solon, Zaleucus, Charondas, and thence to all the Roman edicts and tables with their Justinian;[67] and so down to the Saxon and common laws of England and the statutes.

Sundays also and every evening may be now understandingly spent in the highest matters of theology and church history ancient and modern. And ere this time the Hebrew tongue at a set hour might have been gained, that the Scriptures may be now read in their own original; whereto it would be no impossibility to add the Chaldee and the Syrian dialect.[68] When all these employments are well conquered, then will the choice histories, heroic poems, and Attic tragedies of stateliest and most regal argument, with all the famous political orations, offer themselves; which, if they were not only read but some of them got by memory and solemnly pronounced with right accent and grace, as might be taught, would endue them even with the spirit and vigor of Demosthenes or Cicero, Euripides or Sophocles.

And now, lastly, will be the time to read with them those organic[69] arts which enable men to discourse and write perspicuously, elegantly, and according to the fitted style of lofty, mean,[70] or lowly. Logic therefore, so much as is useful, is to be referred to this due place with all her well-couched[71] heads and topics, until it be time to open her contracted palm into a graceful and ornate rhetoric taught out of the rule of Plato, Aristotle, Phalereus, Cicero, Hermogenes, Longinus. To which poetry would be made subse-

---

[65] best warrant as being inspired  [66] lawgivers respectively of Sparta, Athens, Locri, and Catana in Sicily  [67] edicts . . . Justinian The Twelve Tables or early codification in the fifth century B.C., the edicts issued by the praetors or judges, and the final codification by the emperor Justinian in the sixth century A.D.  [68] dialect Aramaic or spoken Hebrew  [69] organic instrumental  [70] mean medium  [71] well-couched precise

quent, or indeed rather precedent, as being less subtle and fine, but more simple, sensuous, and passionate. I mean not here the prosody of a verse, which they could not but have hit on before among the rudiments of grammar, but that sublime art which in Aristotle's poetics, in Horace, and the Italian commentaries[72] of Castelvetro, Tasso, Mazzoni, and others, teaches what the laws of a true epic poem, what of a dramatic, what of a lyric, what decorum[73] is, which is the grand masterpiece[74] to observe. This would make them soon perceive what despicable creatures our common rhymers and play-writers be, and show them what religious, what glorious and magnificent use might be made of poetry, both in divine and human things.

From hence, and not till now, will be the right season of forming them to be able writers and composers in every excellent matter, when they shall be thus fraught with an universal insight into things. Or whether they be to speak in parliament or council, honor and attention would be waiting on their lips. There would then also appear in pulpits other visages, other gestures, and stuff otherwise wrought than what we now sit under, ofttimes to as great a trial of our patience as any other that they preach to us. These are the studies wherein our noble and our gentle youth ought to bestow their time, in a disciplinary way, from twelve to one-and-twenty: unless they rely more upon their ancestors dead than upon themselves living. In which methodical course it is so supposed they must proceed by the steady pace of learning onward, as at convenient times, for memory's sake, to retire back into the middle-ward,[75] and sometimes into the rear of what they have been taught, until they have confirmed and solidly united the whole body of their perfected knowledge, like the last embattling of a Roman legion.

Now will be worth the seeing what exercises and recreations may best agree and become these studies.

---

[72] commentaries respectively on Aristotle's *Poetics*, epic poetry, and Dante   [73] decorum suitability   [74] masterpiece chief excellence   [75] middle-ward one of the three main divisions of an army: rear-, middle-, and van-guard

The course of study hitherto briefly described is, what I can guess by reading, likest to those ancient and famous schools of Pythagoras, Plato, Isocrates, Aristotle, and such others, out of which were bred up such a number of renowned philosophers, orators, historians, poets, and princes all over Greece, Italy, and Asia, besides the flourishing studies[76] of Cyrene and Alexandria. But herein it shall exceed them and supply a defect as great as that which Plato noted in the commonwealth of Sparta: whereas that city trained up their youth most for war, and these in their academies and Lyceum all for the gown,[77] this institution of breeding which I here delineate shall be equally good both for peace and war. Therefore about an hour and a half ere they eat at noon should be allowed them for exercise and due rest afterwards; but the time for this may be enlarged at pleasure, according as their rising in the morning shall be early.

The exercise which I commend first is the exact use of their weapon, to guard and to strike safely with edge or point. This will keep them healthy, nimble, strong, and well in breath; is also the likeliest means to make them grow large and tall, and to inspire them with a gallant and fearless courage, which being tempered with seasonable lectures and precepts to them of true fortitude and patience, will turn into a native and heroic valor, and make them hate the cowardice of doing wrong. They must be also practiced in all the locks and grips of wrestling, wherein Englishmen were wont to excel, as need may often be in fight to tug, to grapple, and to close. And this perhaps will be enough wherein to prove and heat their single strength.

The interim of unsweating[78] themselves regularly, and convenient rest before meat, may both with profit and delight be taken up in recreating and composing their travailed spirits with the solemn and divine harmonies of music, heard or learned;[79] either while the skilful organist plies his grave and fancied descant[80] in lofty fugues, or the whole

---

[76] studies schools    [77] gown toga, the dress of peace    [78] unsweating cooling off after exercise    [79] heard or learned merely listened to or actually practiced    [80] descant variations on a theme

symphony[81] with artful and unimaginable touches adorn
and grace the well-studied chords of some choice composer;
sometimes the lute or soft organ-stop waiting on elegant
voices, either to religious, martial, or civil ditties; which,
if wise men and prophets be not extremely out, have a
great power over dispositions and manners, to smooth and
make them gentle from rustic harshness and distempered
passions. The like also would not be unexpedient after meat,
to assist and cherish nature in her first concoction,[82] and
send their minds back to study in good tune and satisfaction. Where having followed it close under vigilant eyes
till about two hours before supper, they are, by a sudden
alarum or watchword, to be called out to their military
motions, under sky or covert, according to the season, as
was the Roman wont; first on foot, then, as their age per-
mits, on horseback, to all the art of cavalry; that having in
sport, but with much exactness and daily muster, served
out the rudiments of their soldiership in all the skill of embattling, marching, encamping, fortifying, besieging, and
battering, with all the helps of ancient and modern stratagems, tactics, and warlike maxims, they may as it were
out of a long war come forth renowned and perfect com-
manders in the service of their country. They would not
then, if they were trusted with fair and hopeful armies,
suffer them for want of just and wise discipline to shed
away from about them like sick feathers, though they be
never so oft supplied. They would not suffer their empty
and unrecruitable[83] colonels of twenty men in a company
to quaff out, or convey into secret hoards, the wages of a
delusive list and a miserable remnant;[84] yet in the meanwhile to be overmastered with a score or two of drunkards,
the only soldiery left about them, or else to comply with
all rapines and violences. No, certainly; if they knew aught
of that knowledge that belongs to good men or good governors, they would not suffer these things.

[81] **symphony** orchestra or chorus    [82] **first concoction** first stages of
digestion    [83] **unrecruitable** not able to get recruits    [84] **delusive**
. . . **remnant** a padded company-roll of which the soldiers actually in service were a miserable remnant

But to return to our own institute: besides these constant exercises at home, there is another opportunity of gaining experience to be won from pleasure itself abroad. In those vernal seasons of the year when the air is calm and pleasant, it were an injury and sullenness against nature not to go out and see her riches, and partake in her rejoicing with heaven and earth. I should not therefore be a persuader to them of studying much then, after two or three year that they have well laid their grounds, but to ride out in companies, with prudent and staid guides, to all the quarters of the land: learning and observing all places of strength, all commodities[85] of building and of soil, for towns and tillage, harbors and ports for trade; sometimes taking sea as far as to our navy, to learn there also what they can in the practical knowledge of sailing and of sea-fight.

These ways would try all their peculiar gifts of nature, and if there were any secret excellence among them, would fetch it out and give it fair opportunities to advance itself by, which could not but mightily redound to the good of this nation and bring into fashion again those old admired virtues and excellencies, with far more advantage now in this purity of Christian knowledge. Nor shall we then need the monsieurs of Paris to take our hopeful youth into their slight and prodigal [86] custodies, and send them over back again transformed into mimics, apes, and kickshaws.[87] But if they desire to see other countries at three- or four-and-twenty years of age, not to learn principles, but to enlarge experience and make wise observation, they will by that time be such as shall deserve the regard and honor of all men where they pass, and the society and friendship of those in all places who are best and most eminent. And perhaps then other nations will be glad to visit us for their breeding, or else to imitate us in their own country.

Now, lastly, for their diet there cannot be much to say, save only that it would be best in the same house; for much time else would be lost abroad and many ill habits got. And that it should be plain, healthful, and moderate, I sup-

---

[85] commodities advantages or utilities   [86] slight and prodigal trifling and wasteful   [87] kickshaws frivolous persons

pose is out of controversy. Thus, Master Hartlib, you have a
general view in writing, as your desire was, of that which
at several times I had discoursed with you concerning the
best and noblest way of education; not beginning, as some
have done, from the cradle, which yet might be worth
many considerations if brevity had not been my scope.[88]
Many other circumstances also I could have mentioned, but
this, to such as have the worth in them to make trial, for
light and direction may be enough. Only I believe that this
is not a bow for every man to shoot in[89] that counts himself
a teacher, but will require sinews almost equal to those
which Homer gave Ulysses; yet I am withal persuaded that
it may prove much more easy in the assay,[90] than it now
seems at distance, and much more illustrious; howbeit, not
more difficult than I imagine, and that imagination presents
me with nothing but very happy and very possible according to best wishes, if God have so decreed, and this age
have spirit and capacity enough to apprehend.

[88] scope aim   [89] in with   [90] assay experiment

# AUTOBIOGRAPHICAL PASSAGES
# FROM OTHER PROSE WORKS

FROM *The Reason of Church-Government*
*Urged against Prelaty*, 1642 [1]

For surely to every good and peaceable man it must in
nature needs be a hateful thing to be the displeaser and
molester of thousands; much better would it like him
doubtless to be the messenger of gladness and contentment, which is his chief intended business, to all mankind,
but that they resist and oppose their own true happiness.
But when God commands to take the trumpet and blow a
dolorous or a jarring blast, it lies not in man's will what he
shall say or what he shall conceal. If he shall think to be
silent, as Jeremiah[2] did, because of the reproach and deri-
sion he met with daily, and "all his familiar friends watched
for his halting," to be revenged on him for speaking the
truth, he would be forced to confess as he confessed: "His
word was in my heart as a burning fire shut up in my bones;
I was weary with forebearing, and could not stay." Which
might teach these times not suddenly to condemn all things
that are sharply spoken or vehemently written as proceeding
out of stomach,[3] virulence, and ill nature; but to consider
rather that if the prelates have leave to say the worst that
can be said, and do the worst that can be done, while they
strive to keep to themselves, to their great pleasure and
commodity, those things which they ought to render up,
no man can be justly offended with him that will endeavor

---

[1] The Columbia Milton, Vol. III, Part I, p. 231   [2] *Jeremiah* xx,
9-10   [3] stomach malice or spite

73

to impart and bestow, without any gain to himself, those
sharp but saving words which would be a terror and a tor-
ment in him to keep back.

For me, I have determined to lay up as the best treasure
and solace of a good old age, if God vouchsafe it to me, the
honest liberty of free speech from my youth, where I shall
think it available in so dear a concernment as the church's
good. For if I be, either by disposition or what other cause,
too inquisitive,[4] or suspicious[5] of myself and mine own do-
ings, who can help it? But this I foresee, that should the
church be brought under heavy oppression, and God have
given me ability the while to reason against that man that
should be the author of so foul a deed; or should she, by
blessing from above on the industry and courage of faithful
men, change this her distracted estate into better days without the least furtherance or contribution of those few talents
which God at that present had lent me; I foresee what
stories I should hear within myself, all my life after, of discourage and reproach. "Timorous and ingrateful, the church
of God is now again at the foot of her insulting enemies,
and thou bewailest. What matters it for thee or thy bewail-
ing? When time was, thou couldst not find a syllable of all
that thou hadst read, or studied, to utter in her behalf. Yet
ease and leisure was given thee for thy retired thoughts out
of the sweat of other men. Thou hadst the diligence, the
parts, the language of a man, if a vain subject were to be
adorned or beautified; but when the cause of God and His
church was to be pleaded, for which purpose that tongue
was given thee which thou hast, God listened if He could
hear thy voice among His zealous servants, but thou wert
dumb as a beast; from henceforward be that which thine
own brutish silence hath made thee." Or else I should have
heard on the other ear: "Slothful and ever to be set light
by, the church hath now overcome her late distresses after
the unwearied labors of many her true servants that stood
up in her defense; thou also wouldst take upon thee to share
amongst them of their joy: but wherefore thou? Where
canst thou show any word or deed of thine which might

[4] **inquisitive** curious or inquiring   [5] **suspicious** distrustful

have hastened her peace? Whatever thou dost now talk, or write, or look, is the alms of other men's active prudence and zeal. Dare not now to say or do anything better than thy former sloth and infancy;[6] or if thou darest, thou dost impudently to make a thrifty purchase of boldness to thyself out of the painful merits of other men; what before was thy sin is now thy duty to be, abject and worthless." These and such like lessons as these I know would have been my matins duly and my evensong.[7] But now by this little diligence mark what a privilege I have gained with good men and saints to claim my right of lamenting the tribulations of the church, if she should suffer, when others that have ventured nothing for her sake have not the honor to be admitted mourners. But if she lift up her drooping head and prosper, among those that have something more than wished her welfare I have my charter and freehold of rejoicing to me and my heirs.

Concerning therefore this wayward [8] subject against prelaty, the touching whereof is so distasteful and disquietous to a number of men, as by what has been said I may deserve of charitable readers to be credited that neither envy nor gall hath entered me upon this controversy, but the enforcement of conscience only, and a preventive[9] fear lest the omitting of this duty should be against me, when I would store up to myself the good provision of peaceful hours; so, lest it should be still imputed to me, as I have found it hath been, that some self-pleasing humor of vainglory hath incited me to contest with men of high estimation now while green years[10] are upon my head, from this needless surmisal I shall hope to dissuade the intelligent and equal [11] auditor, if I can but say successfully that which in this exigent[12] behooves me; although I would be heard only, if it might be, by the elegant and learned reader, to whom principally for a while I shall beg leave I may address myself. To him it will be no new thing though I tell

[6] infancy speechlessness   [7] matins . . . evensong my rightful lesson morning and evening   [8] wayward untoward   [9] preventive anticipatory   [10] years Milton was thirty-three   [11] equal impartial   [12] exigent emergency

him that if I hunted after praise by the ostentation of wit
and learning, I should not write thus out of mine own season, when I have neither yet completed to my mind the full
circle of my private studies, although I complain not of any
insufficiency to the matter in hand; or were I ready to my
wishes, it were a folly to commit anything elaborately composed to the careless and interrupted listening of these tu-
multuous times. Next, if I were wise only to mine own ends,
I would certainly take such a subject as of itself might catch
applause—whereas this hath all the disadvantages on the
contrary—and such a subject as the publishing whereof
might be delayed at pleasure, and time enough to pencil it
over with all the curious touches of art, even to the perfection of a faultless picture; whenas in this argument the not
deferring is of great moment to the good speeding,[13] that
if solidity have leisure to do her office, art cannot have
much.[14] Lastly, I should not choose this manner of writing,[15] wherein knowing myself inferior to myself, led by the
genial power of nature[16] to another task, I have the use, as
I may account it, but of my left hand. And though I shall
be foolish in saying more to this purpose, yet, since it will
be such folly as wisest men going about to commit have
only confessed and so committed, I may trust with more
reason, because with more folly, to have courteous pardon.
For although a poet, soaring in the high region of his fancies
with his garland and singing robes about him, might without apology speak more for himself than I mean to do, yet
for me sitting here below in the cool element of prose, a
mortal thing among many readers of no empyreal conceit,[17]
to venture and divulge unusual things of myself, I shall
petition to the gentler sort, it may not be envy[18] to me.

I must say therefore that after I had from my first
years, by the ceaseless diligence and care of my father
(whom God recompense), been exercised to the tongues
and some sciences, as my age would suffer, by sundry mas-

[13] good speeding success   [14] solidity . . . much if the argument
is made solid, there is not much time to adorn the style   [15] writing i.e., in prose   [16] genial . . . nature natural inclination
[17] mortal . . . conceit by many deemed unfit for elevated writing   [18] envy occasion of odium

ters and teachers both at home and at the schools, it was found that whether aught was imposed me by them that had the overlooking, or betaken to of mine own choice, in English or other tongue, prosing or versing but chiefly this latter, the style, by certain vital signs it had, was likely to live. But much latelier in the private academies of Italy, whither I was favored to resort, perceiving that some trifles which I had in memory, composed at under twenty or thereabout (for the manner is that everyone must give some proof of his wit and reading there), met with acceptance above what was looked for; and other things, which I had shifted [19] in scarcity of books and conveniences to patch up amongst them, were received with written encomiums, which the Italian is not forward to bestow on men of this side the Alps; I began thus far to assent to them and divers of my friends here at home, and not less to an inward prompting which now grew daily upon me, that by labor and intent study (which I take to be my portion in this life) joined with the strong propensity of nature, I might perhaps leave something so written to aftertimes as they should not willingly let it die.

These thoughts at once possessed me, and these other: that if I were certain to write as men buy leases, for three lives and downward,[20] there ought no regard be sooner had than to God's glory by the honor and instruction of my country. For which cause, and not only for that[21] I knew it would be hard to arrive at the second rank among the Latins, I applied myself to that resolution which Ariosto followed against the persuasions of Bembo,[22] to fix all the industry and art I could unite to the adorning of my native tongue; not to make verbal curiosities the end (that were a toilsome vanity) but to be an interpreter and relater of the best and sagest things among mine own citizens throughout this island in the mother dialect: that what the greatest and choicest wits of Athens, Rome, or modern Italy,

[19] shifted managed  [20] leases . . . downward enduring for a long time  [21] for that because  [22] Ariosto . . . Bembo being an enthusiastic Latinist Cardinal Bembo advised the poet Ariosto not to write in Italian

and those Hebrews of old did for their country, I in my proportion, with this over and above of being a Christian, might do for mine; not caring to be once named abroad, though perhaps I could attain to that, but content with these British Islands as my world; whose fortune hath hitherto been, that if the Athenians, as some say, made their small deeds great and renowned by their eloquent writers, England hath had her noble achievements made small by the unskilful handling of monks and mechanics.

Time serves not now, and perhaps I might seem too profuse, to give any certain account of what the mind at home, in the spacious circuits of her musing, hath liberty to propose to herself, though of highest hope and hardest attempting; whether that epic form whereof the two poems of Homer and those other two of Virgil and Tasso are a diffuse, and the book of Job a brief model: or whether the rules of Aristotle herein are strictly to be kept or nature to be followed, which in them that know art and use judgment is no transgression but an enriching of art: and lastly, what king or knight before the conquest might be chosen in whom to lay the pattern of a Christian hero. And as Tasso gave to a prince of Italy his choice whether he would command him to write of Godfrey's expedition against the infidels, or Belisarius against the Goths, or Charlemagne against the Lombards; if to the instinct of nature and the emboldening of art aught can be trusted, and that there be nothing adverse in our climate, or the fate of this age, it haply would be no rashness, from an equal diligence and inclination, to present the like offer in our own ancient stories.[23] Or whether those dramatic constitutions,[24] wherein Sophocles and Euripides reign, shall be found more doctrinal and exemplary[25] to a nation, the Scripture also affords us a divine pastoral drama in the Song of Solomon, consisting of two persons and a double chorus, as Origen rightly judges. And the Apocalypse of Saint John is the majestic image of a high and stately tragedy, shutting up and intermingling her solemn scenes and acts with a sevenfold chorus of

[23] stories    histories    [24] constitutions    compositions    [25] doctrinal
. . . exemplary    instructive and worthy of imitation

hallelujahs and harping symphonies: and this my opinion
the grave authority of Pareus,[26] commenting that book, is
sufficient to confirm. Or if occasion shall lead to imitate
those magnific odes and hymns, wherein Pindarus and Calli-
machus are in most things worthy, some others in their
frame[27] judicious, in their matter most an end [28] faulty. But
those frequent songs throughout the law and prophets beyond all these, not in their divine argument alone but in
the very critical art of composition, may be easily made to
appear over all kinds of lyric poesy to be incomparable.

These abilities, wheresoever they be found, are the inspired gift of God rarely bestowed, but yet to some (though
most abuse) in every nation; and are of power beside[29]
the office of a pulpit to inbreed and cherish in a great people the seeds of virtue and public civility; to allay the per-
turbations of the mind and set the affections in right tune
to celebrate in glorious and lofty hymns the throne and
equipage of God's almightiness, and what He works, and
what He suffers to be wrought with high providence in His
church; to sing the victorious agonies of martyrs and saints,
the deeds and triumphs of just and pious nations doing
valiantly through faith against the enemies of Christ; to
deplore the general relapses of kingdoms and states from
justice and God's true worship. Lastly, whatsoever in religion is holy and sublime, in virtue amiable or grave, whatsoever hath passion or admiration[30] in all the changes of that
which is called fortune from without, or the wily subtleties
and refluxes[31] of man's thoughts from within; all these
things with a solid and treatable smoothness to paint out
and describe, teaching over the whole book of sanctity and
virtue, through all the instances of example, with such delight to those especially of soft and delicious[32] temper, who
will not so much as look upon Truth herself unless they see
her elegantly dressed, that whereas the paths of honesty
and good life appear now rugged and difficult, though they

---

[26] Pareus David (1548-1622) professor of theology at Heidelberg
[27] frame form  [28] most an end for the most part  [29] beside com-
parable with  [30] admiration wonder  [31] refluxes ebb and flow
[32] delicious fastidious

be indeed easy and pleasant, they would then appear to all men both easy and pleasant, though they were rugged and difficult indeed. And what a benefit this would be to our youth and gentry may soon be guessed by what we know of the corruption and bane which they suck in daily from the writings and interludes of libidinous and ignorant poetasters, who have scarce ever heard of that which is the main consistence of a true poem, the choice of such persons as they ought to introduce, and what is moral and decent to each one; do for the most part lap up vicious principles in sweet pills to be swallowed down, and make the taste of virtuous documents[33] harsh and sour.

But because the spirit of man cannot demean itself lively in this body without some recreating intermission of labor and serious things, it were happy for the commonwealth if our magistrates, as in those famous governments of old, would take into their care not only the deciding of our contentious law-cases and brawls, but the managing of our public sports and festival pastimes; that they might be not such as were authorized a while since, the provocations of drunkenness and lust, but such as may inure and harden our bodies by martial exercises to all warlike skill and performance, and may civilize, adorn, and make discreet our minds by the learned and affable meeting of frequent academies and the procurement of wise and artful [34] recitations, sweetened with graceful and eloquent enticements to the love and practice of justice, temperance, and fortitude, instructing and bettering the nation at all opportunities; that the call of wisdom and virtue may be heard everywhere, as Solomon saith, "She crieth without, she uttereth her voice in the streets, in the top of high places, in the chief concourse, and in the openings of the gates." Whether this may not be, not only in pulpits but after another persuasive method, at set and solemn panegyries[35] in theaters, porches, or what other place or way may win most upon the people to receive at once both recreation and instruction, let them in authority consult.

---

[33] documents lessons   [34] artful artistic   [35] panegyries assemblies

The thing which I had to say, and those intentions which have lived within me ever since I could conceive myself anything worth to my country, I return to crave excuse that urgent reason hath plucked from me by an abortive and foredated discovery.[36] And the accomplishment of them lies not but in a power above man's to promise; but that none hath by more studious ways endeavored, and with more unwearied spirit that none shall, that I dare almost aver of myself, as far as life and free leisure will extend, and that[37] the land had once enfranchised herself from this impertinent yoke of prelaty, under whose inquisitorious and tyrannical duncery no free and splendid wit can flourish. Neither do I think it shame to covenant with any knowing reader that for some few years yet I may go on trust with him toward the payment of what I am now indebted, as being a work not to be raised from the heat of youth or the vapors of wine, like that which flows at waste[38] from the pen of some vulgar amorist, or the trencher fury of a rhyming parasite, nor to be obtained by the invocation of Dame Memory and her siren daughters, but by devout prayer to that eternal Spirit who can enrich with all utterance and knowledge, and sends out His seraphim, with the hallowed fire of His altar, to touch and purify the lips of whom He pleases: to this must be added industrious and select reading, steady observation, insight into all seemly and generous arts and affairs; till which in some measure be compassed, at mine own peril and cost I refuse not to sustain this expectation from as many as are not loath to hazard so much credulity upon the best pledges that I can give them.

Although it nothing content me to have disclosed thus much beforehand, but that I trust hereby to make it manifest with what small willingness I endure to interrupt the pursuit of no less hopes than these, and leave a calm and pleasant solitariness fed with cheerful and confident thoughts, to embark in a troubled sea of noises and hoarse disputes, put from beholding the bright countenance of

[36] abortive . . . discovery premature disclosure before accomplishment  [37] and that if  [38] at waste uselessly

Truth in the quiet and still air of delightful studies to come
into the dim reflection of hollow antiquities sold by the
seeming bulk, and there be fain to club quotations with
men whose learning and belief lies in marginal stuffings,
who when they have like good sumpters[39] laid ye down
their horseload of citations and fathers at your door, with
a rhapsody of who and who were bishops here or there, ye
may take off their packsaddles, their day's work is done,
and episcopacy, as they think, stoutly vindicated. Let any
gentle apprehension that can distinguish learned pains
from unlearned drudgery imagine what pleasure or pro-
foundness can be in this, or what honor to deal against such
adversaries. But were it the meanest underservice, if God
by His secretary conscience enjoin it, it were sad for me if
I should draw back; for me especially, now when all men
offer their aid to help ease and lighten the difficult labors
of the church, to whose service, by the intentions of my
parents and friends, I was destined of a child, and in mine
own resolutions; till coming to some maturity of years and
perceiving what tyranny had invaded the church, that he
who would take orders must subscribe slave, and take an
oath withal, which, unless he took with a conscience that
would retch, he must either straight perjure or split his
faith; I thought it better to prefer a blameless silence before
the sacred office of speaking, bought and begun with servitude and forswearing. Howsoever, thus church-outed by
the prelates, hence may appear the right I have to meddle
in these matters, as before the necessity and constraint
appeared.

[39] sumpters pack-animals

### from *An Apology against a Pamphlet Called a Modest Confutation of the Animadversions upon the Remonstrant against Smectymnuus*, 1642[1]

Thus having spent his[2] first onset not in confuting but
in a reasonless defaming of the book, the method of his
malice hurries him to attempt the like against the author;
not by proofs and testimonies, but "having no certain notice
of me," as he professes, "further than what he gathers from
the *Animadversions*," blunders at me for the rest, and
flings out stray crimes at a venture which he could never,
though he be a serpent, suck from anything that I have
written, but from his own stuffed magazine and hoard of
slanderous inventions, over and above that which he converted to venom in the drawing. To me, readers, it happens
as a singular contentment, and let it be to good men no
slight satisfaction, that the slanderer here confesses he has
"no further notice of me than his own conjecture." Although
it had been honest to have inquired before he uttered such
infamous words; and I am credibly informed he did inquire,
but finding small comfort from the intelligence which he
received whereon to ground the falsities which he had
provided, thought it his likeliest course, under a pretended
ignorance, to let drive at random, lest he should lose his
odd ends which from some penurious book of characters[3]
he had been culling out and would fain apply: not caring[4]
to burden me with those vices whereof, among whom my

---

[1] The Columbia Milton, Vol. III, Part I, p. 295   [2] his the anonymous author of the *Modest Confutation*   [3] characters containing short sketches of type-personalities   [4] not caring being indifferent

conversation[5] hath been, I have been ever least suspected; perhaps not without some subtlety to cast me into envy[6] by bringing on me a necessity to enter into mine own praises. In which argument I know every wise man is more unwillingly drawn to speak than the most repining ear can be adverse to hear.

Nevertheless, since I dare not wish to pass this life unpersecuted of slanderous tongues, for God hath told us that to be generally praised is woeful, I shall rely on His promise to free the innocent from causeless aspersions: whereof nothing sooner can assure me than if I shall feel Him now assisting me in the just vindication of myself, which yet I could defer, it being more meet that to those other matters of public debatement in this book I should give attendance first, but that I fear it would but harm the truth for me to reason in her behalf, so long as I should suffer my honest estimation to lie unpurged from these insolent suspicions. And if I shall be large or unwonted [7] in justifying myself to those who know me not, for else it would be needless, let them consider that a short slander will ofttimes reach farther than a long apology; and that he who will do justly to all men must begin from knowing how, if it so happen, to be not unjust to himself. I must be thought, if this libeller (for now he shows himself to be so) can find belief, after an inordinate and riotous youth spent at "the University," to have been at length "vomited out thence." For which commodious lie, that he may be encouraged in the trade another time, I thank him; for it hath given me an apt occasion to acknowledge publicly, with all grateful mind, that more than ordinary favor and respect which I found above any of my equals at the hands of those courteous and learned men, the Fellows of that College wherein I spent some years, who at my parting, after I had taken two degrees, as the manner is, signified many ways how much better it would content them that I would stay; as by many letters full of kindness and loving respect, both before that

---

[5] conversation association   [6] envy odium   [7] large or unwonted lengthy or unusual

time and long after, I was assured of their singular good affection towards me. Which being likewise propense[8] to all such as were for their studious and civil life worthy of esteem, I could not wrong their judgments and upright intentions so much as to think I had that regard from them for other cause than that I might be still encouraged to proceed in the honest and laudable courses of which they apprehended I had given good proof. And to those ingenuous and friendly men, who were ever the countenancers of virtuous and hopeful wits, I wish the best and happiest things that friends in absence wish one to another.

As for the common approbation or dislike of that place, as now it is, that I should esteem or disesteem myself or any other the more for that, too simple and too credulous is the confuter, if he think to obtain with[9] me or any right discerner. Of small practice were that physician who could not judge, by what both she or her sister[10] hath of long time vomited, that the worser stuff she strongly keeps in her stomach, but the better she is ever kecking[11] at, and is queasy. She vomits now out of sickness; but ere it be well with her, she must vomit by strong physic. In the meanwhile that "suburb sink," as this rude scavenger calls it, and more than scurriously taunts it with "plague," having a worse plague in his middle entrail, that suburb wherein I dwell shall be in my account a more honorable place than his university. Which as in the time of her better health, and mine own younger judgment, I never greatly admired, so now much less. But he follows me to the city, still usurping and forging beyond his book notice, which only he affirms to have had; "and where my morning haunts are he wisses[12] not." 'Tis wonder that, being so rare an alchemist of slander, he could not extract that, as well as the university vomit and the suburb sink which his art could distil so cunningly; but because his limbec fails him, to give him and envy the more vexation, I'll tell him.

---

[8] propense favorable   [9] obtain with gain a victory over   [10] she . . . sister Cambridge or Oxford   [11] kecking gagging   [12] wisses knows

Those morning haunts are where they should be, at home; not sleeping or concocting[13] the surfeits of an irregular feast, but up and stirring, in winter often ere the sound of any bell awake men to labor or to devotion; in summer as oft with the bird that first arouses, or not much tardier, to read good authors, or cause[14] them to be read, till the attention be weary or memory have his full fraught:[15] then, with useful and generous labors preserving the body's health and hardiness to render lightsome, clear, and not lumpish obedience to the mind, to the cause of religion, and our country's liberty, when it shall require firm hearts in sound bodies to stand and cover[16] their stations, rather than to see the ruin of our protestation and the enforcement of a slavish life. These are the morning practices: proceed now to the afternoon; "in playhouses," he says, "and the bordellos." Your intelligence, unfaithful spy of Canaan? He gives in his evidence[17] that "there he hath traced me." Take him at his word, readers, but let him bring good sureties, ere ye dismiss him, that while he pretended to dog others he did not turn in for his own pleasure: for so much in effect he concludes against himself, not contented to be caught in every other gin,[18] but he must be such a novice as to be still hampered in his own hemp.[19] "In the *Animadversions*," saith he, "I find the mention of old cloaks, false beards, night-walkers, and salt lotion; therefore the animadverter haunts playhouses and bordellos; for if he did not, how could he speak of such gear?" Now that he may know what it is to be a child and yet to meddle with edged tools, I turn his antistrophon[20] upon his own head; the confuter knows that these things are the furniture of playhouses and bordellos, therefore, by the same reason, the confuter himself hath been traced in those places. Was it such a dissolute speech, telling of some politicians who were wont to eavesdrop in disguises, to say they were often

---

[13] concocting digesting  [14] cause as a teacher; Milton was not yet blind  [15] fraught freight  [16] cover guard  [17] gives . . . evidence testifies  [18] gin snare  [19] hampered . . . hemp tangled in his own rope  [20] antistrophon retort

liable to a night-walking cudgeller or the emptying of a urinal? What if I had writ as your friend the author of the aforesaid mime, *Mundus alter et idem*,[21] to have been ravished like some young Cephalus or Hylas by a troup of camping housewives in Viraginia,[22] and that he was there forced to swear himself an uxorious varlet, then after a long servitude to have come into Aphrodisia that pleasant country, that gave such a sweet smell to his nostrils among the shameless courtesans of Desvergonia? Surely he would then have concluded me as constant at the bordello as the galley-slave at his oar.

But since there is such necessity to the hearsay of a tire, a periwig, or a vizard, that plays must have been seen, what difficulty was there in that, when in the colleges so many of the young divines, and those in next aptitude to divinity, have been seen so often upon the stage, writhing and un-boning their clergy limbs to all the antic and dishonest gestures of Trinculoes, buffoons, and bawds; prostituting the shame of that ministry which either they had, or were nigh having, to the eyes of courtiers and court-ladies, with their grooms and mademoiselles?[23] There, while they acted and overacted, among other young scholars I was a spectator; they thought themselves gallant men, and I thought them fools; they made sport, and I laughed; they mispronounced, and I misliked; and to make up the atticism,[24] they were out,[25] and I hissed. Judge now whether so many good text-men were not sufficient to instruct me of false beards and vizards without more expositors; and how can this confuter take the face to object to me the seeing of that which his reverent prelates allow, and incite their young disciples to act? For if it be unlawful to sit and be-

---

[21] **Mundus . . . idem** "A World Different Yet the Same," a satire, in the form of a fanciful book of travel, by Joseph Hall, whose views of church government were defended against Milton in the *Modest Confutation* [22] Viraginia is the land of the viragoes [23] mademoiselles French maids [24] atticism well-turned phrase [25] out on the stage

hold a mercenary comedian personating that which is least unseemly for a hireling to do, how much more blameful is it to endure the sight of as vile things acted by persons either entered or presently to enter into the ministry; and how much more foul and ignominious for them to be the actors!

But because as well by this upbraiding to me the bordellos as by other suspicious glancing in his book he would seem privily to point me out to his readers as one whose custom of life were not honest but licentious, I shall entreat to be borne with though I digress, and in a way not often trod acquaint ye with the sum of my thoughts in this matter, through the course of my years and studies: although I am not ignorant how hazardous it will be to do this under the nose of the envious, as it were in skirmish to change the compact order, and instead of outward actions, to bring inmost thoughts into front. And I must tell ye, readers, that by this sort of men I have been already bitten at; yet shall they not for me know how slightly they are esteemed, unless they have so much learning as to read what in Greek ἀπειροκαλία[26] is, which, together with envy,[27] is the common disease of those who censure books that are not for their reading. With me it fares now as with him whose outward garment hath been injured and ill bedighted; for having no other shift, what help but to turn the inside outwards, especially if the lining be of the same, or, as it is sometimes, much better? So if my name and outward demeanor be not evident enough to defend me, I must make trial if the discovery of my inmost thoughts can: wherein of two purposes, both honest and both sincere, the one perhaps I shall not miss; although I fail to gain belief with others, of being such as my perpetual thoughts shall here disclose me, I may yet not fail of success in persuading some to be such really themselves, as they cannot believe me to be more than what I feign.

I had my time, readers, as others have who have good learning bestowed upon them, to be sent to those places

---

[26] ἀπειροκαλία lack of taste    [27] envy ill-will

where, the opinion was, it might be soonest attained; and as the manner is, was not unstudied in those authors which are most commended. Whereof some were grave orators and historians, whose matter methought I loved indeed, but as my age then was, so I understood them; others were the smooth elegiac poets, whereof the schools are not scarce,[28] whom both for the pleasing sound of their numerous[29] writing, which in imitation I found most easy and most agreeable to nature's part in me, and for their matter, which what it is there be few who know not, I was so allured to read that no recreation came to me better welcome. For that it was then those years with me which are excused though they be least severe, I may be saved the labor to remember[30] ye. Whence, having observed them to account it the chief glory of their wit in that they were ablest to judge, to praise, and by that could esteem themselves worthiest to love those high perfections which under one or other name they took to celebrate, I thought with myself by every instinct and presage of nature, which is not wont to be false, that what emboldened them to this task might with such diligence as they used embolden me; and that what judgment, wit, or elegance was my share would herein best appear and best value itself, by how much more wisely and with more love of virtue I should choose (let rude ears be absent) the object of not unlike praises. For albeit these thoughts to some will seem virtuous and commendable, to others only pardonable, to a third sort perhaps idle, yet the mentioning of them now will end in serious.[31]

Nor blame it, readers, in those years[32] to propose to themselves such a reward as the noblest dispositions above other things in this life have sometimes preferred: whereof not to be sensible, when good and fair in one person meet, argues both a gross and shallow judgment, and withal an ungentle and swainish[33] breast. For by the firm settling of

---

[28] scarce deficient [29] numerous in verse [30] remember remind [31] end in serious lead to something important [32] blame . . . years censure one of that age [33] swainish boorish

these persuasions I became, to my best memory, so much a proficient that if I found those authors anywhere speaking unworthy things of themselves, or unchaste of those names which before they had extolled, this effect it wrought with me: from that time forward their art I still applauded, but the men I deplored; and above them all preferred the two famous renowners[34] of Beatrice and Laura, who never write but honor of them to whom they devote their verse, displaying sublime and pure thoughts without transgression. And long it was not after when I was confirmed in this opinion, that he who would not be frustrate of his hope to write well hereafter in laudable things ought himself to be a true poem; that is, a composition and pattern of the best and honorablest things; not presuming to sing high praises of heroic men or famous cities, unless he have in himself the experience and the practice of all that which is praiseworthy. These reasonings, together with a certain niceness[35] of nature, an honest haughtiness, and self-esteem either of what I was or what I might be (which let envy call pride), and lastly that modesty, whereof, though not in the title-page,[36] yet here I may be excused to make some beseeming profession; all these uniting the supply of their natural aid together, kept me still above those low descents of mind beneath which he must deject and plunge himself that can agree to salable and unlawful prostitutions.

Next (for hear me out now, readers, that I may tell ye whither my younger feet wandered), I betook me among those lofty fables and romances which recount in solemn cantos the deeds of knighthood founded by our victorious kings, and from hence had in renown over all Christendom. There I read it in the oath of every knight that he should defend to the expense of his best blood, or of his life if it so befell him, the honor and chastity of virgin or matron; from whence even then I learned what a noble virtue chastity needs must be, to the defense of which so many worthies, by such a dear adventure of themselves, had sworn. And if I found in the story afterward any of them, by word

---

[34] **renowners** Dante and Petrarch   [35] **niceness** delicacy   [36] **title-page** an ironical reference to the *Modest Confutation*

or deed, breaking that oath, I judged it the same fault of the poet as that which is attributed to Homer,[37] to have written undecent things of the gods. Only this my mind gave me, that every free and gentle spirit, without that oath, ought to be born a knight, nor needed to expect[38] the gilt spur or the laying of a sword upon his shoulder to stir him up both by his counsel and his arm to secure and protect the weakness of any attempted chastity. So that even those books, which to many others have been the fuel of wantonness and loose living, I cannot think how unless by divine indulgence, proved to me so many incitements, as you have heard, to the love and steadfast observation of that virtue which abhors the society of bordellos.

Thus, from the laureate fraternity of poets, riper years and the ceaseless round of study and reading led me to the shady spaces of philosophy, but chiefly to the divine volumes of Plato[39] and his equal Xenophon: where if I should tell ye what I learned of chastity and love (I mean that which is truly so, whose charming cup is only virtue which she bears in her hand to those who are worthy—the rest are cheated with a thick intoxicating potion which a certain sorceress, the abuser of love's name, carries about) and how the first and chiefest office of love begins and ends in the soul, producing those happy twins of her divine generation, knowledge and virtue, with such abstracted sublimities as these, it might be worth your listening, readers, as I may one day hope to have ye in a still time, when there shall be no chiding; not in these noises, the adversary as you know barking at the door, or searching for me at the bordellos where it may be he has lost himself, and raps up without pity the sage and rheumatic old prelatess, with all her young Corinthian laity, to inquire for such a one.

Last of all, not in time but as perfection is last, that care was ever had of me, with my earliest capacity, not to be negligently trained in the precepts of Christian religion: this that I have hitherto related hath been to show that

[37] Homer by Plato; *Republic* 381 D    [38] expect await    [39] Plato
See Socrates's speech in *Symposium* 201 D ff.

though Christianity had been but slightly taught me, yet a certain reservedness of natural disposition, and moral discipline learned out of the noblest philosophy, was enough to keep me in disdain of far less incontinences than this of the bordello. But having had the doctrine of Holy Scripture unfolding those chaste and high mysteries with timeliest care infused, that "the body is for the Lord, and the Lord for the body," thus also I argued to myself, that if unchastity in a woman, whom Saint Paul terms the glory of man, be such a scandal and dishonor, then certainly in a man, who is both the image and glory of God, it must, though commonly not so thought, be much more deflowering and dishonorable; in that he sins both against his own body, which is the perfecter sex, and his own glory, which is in the woman; and that which is worst, against the image and glory of God, which is in himself. Nor did I slumber over that place expressing such high rewards of ever accompanying the Lamb with those celestial songs to others inapprehensible, but not to those who were not defiled with women, which doubtless means fornication; for marriage must not be called a defilement.

## FROM *The Second Defense of The People of England*, 1654[1]

A grateful recollection of the divine goodness is the first of human obligations; and extraordinary favors demand more solemn and devout acknowledgments: with such acknowledgments I feel it my duty to begin this work. First, because I was born at a time when the virtue of my fellow-citizens, far exceeding that of their progenitors in greatness of soul and vigor of enterprise, having invoked Heaven to witness the justice of their cause and been clearly governed by its directions, has succeeded in delivering the commonwealth from the most grievous tyranny and religion from the most ignominious degradation. And next, because when there suddenly arose many who, as is usual with the vulgar, basely calumniated the most illustrious achievements, and when one eminent above the rest, inflated with literary pride and the zealous applauses of his partisans, had in a scandalous publication, which was particularly levelled against me, nefariously undertaken to plead the cause of despotism, I, who was neither deemed unequal to so renowned an adversary nor to so great a subject, was particularly selected by the deliverers of our country, and by the general suffrage of the public, openly to vindicate the rights of the English nation and consequently of liberty itself.[2] Lastly, because in a matter of so much moment, and which excited such ardent expectations, I did not disappoint the hopes nor the opinions of my fellow-citizens; while men of

[1] English translation by Robert Fellowes. The Bohn Edition of the *Prose Works of John Milton*, Vol. I, p. 216   [2] to vindicate . . . itself in *A Defense of the People of England in Answer to Salmasius's Defense of the King*, 1651

learning and eminence abroad honored me with unmingled approbation; while I obtained such a victory over my opponent that, notwithstanding his unparalleled assurance, he was obliged to quit the field with his courage broken and his reputation lost; and for the three years which he lived afterwards, much as he menaced and furiously as he raved, he gave me no further trouble, except that he procured the paltry aid of some despicable hirelings and suborned some of his silly and extravagant admirers to support him under the weight of the unexpected and recent disgrace which he had experienced. This will immediately appear. Such are the signal favors which I ascribe to the divine beneficence, and which I thought it right devoutly to commemorate, not only that I might discharge a debt of gratitude, but particularly because they seem auspicious to the success of my present undertaking. For who is there who does not identify the honor of his country with his own? And what can conduce more to the beauty or glory of one's country than the recovery not only of its civil but its religious liberty? And what nation or state ever obtained both by more successful or more valorous exertion? For fortitude is seen resplendent not only in the field of battle and amid the clash of arms, but displays its energy under every difficulty and against every assailant.

Relying on the divine assistance, they [the English people] used every honorable exertion to break the yoke of slavery; of the praise of which, though I claim no share to myself, yet I can easily repel any charge which may be adduced against me, either of want of courage or want of zeal. For though I did not participate in the toils or dangers of the war, yet I was at the same time engaged in a service not less hazardous to myself and more beneficial to my fellow-citizens; nor, in the adverse turns of our affairs, did I ever betray any symptoms of pusillanimity and dejection, or show myself more afraid than became me of malice or of death. For since from my youth I was devoted to the pursuits of literature, and my mind had always been stronger than my body, I did not court the labors of a camp,

in which any common person would have been of more
service than myself, but resorted to that employment in
which my exertions were likely to be of most avail. Thus,
with the better part of my frame I contributed as much as
possible to the good of my country, and to the success of
the glorious cause in which we were engaged; and I thought
that if God willed the success of such glorious achievements, it was equally agreeable to his will that there should
be others by whom those achievements should be recorded
with dignity and elegance; and that the truth, which had
been defended by arms, should also be defended by reason,
which is the best and only legitimate means of defending
it. Hence, while I applaud those who were victorious in
the field, I will not complain of the province which was
assigned me; but rather congratulate myself upon it, and
thank the Author of all good for having placed me in a
station which may be an object of envy to others rather
than of regret to myself. I am far from wishing to make any
vain or arrogant comparisons or to speak ostentatiously of
myself; but in a cause so great and glorious, and particularly
on an occasion when I am called by the general suffrage to
defend the very defenders of that cause, I can hardly re-
frain from assuming a more lofty and swelling tone than
the simplicity of an exordium may seem to justify; and
much as I may be surpassed in the powers of eloquence and
copiousness of diction by the illustrious orators of antiquity,
yet the subject of which I treat was never surpassed in any
age, in dignity or in interest.

Let us now come to the charges which were brought
against myself.[3] Is there anything reprehensible in my
manners or my conduct? Surely nothing. What no one not
totally divested of all generous sensibility would have done,
he reproaches me with want of beauty and loss of sight.
"A monster huge and hideous, void of sight." I certainly

[3] charges . . . myself in "The Cry of the King's Blood against
the English Parricides," which Milton is answering. He supposed, erroneously, that it had been written by Alexander More

never supposed that I should have been obliged to enter
into a competition for beauty with the Cyclops; but he
immediately corrects himself and says, "though not indeed
huge, for there cannot be a more spare, shrivelled, and
bloodless form." It is of no moment to say anything of personal appearance, yet lest (as the Spanish vulgar, implicitly
confiding in the relations of their priests, believe of heretics)
anyone, from the representations of my enemies, should
be led to imagine that I have either the head of a dog or
the horn of a rhinoceros, I will say something on the subject, that I may have an opportunity of paying my grateful
acknowledgments to the Deity, and of refuting the most
shameless lies. I do not believe that I was ever once noted
for deformity by any one who ever saw me; but the praise
of beauty I am not anxious to obtain. My stature certainly
is not tall; but it rather approaches the middle than the
diminutive. Yet what if it were diminutive, when so many
men, illustrious both in peace and war, have been the
same? And how can that be called diminutive which is
great enough for every virtuous achievement? Nor, though
very thin, was I ever deficient in courage or in strength;
and I was wont constantly to exercise myself in the use of
the broadsword, as long as it comported with my habit and
my years. Armed with this weapon, as I usually was, I
should have thought myself quite a match for anyone,
though much stronger than myself; and I felt perfectly
secure against the assault of any open enemy. At this moment I have the same courage, the same strength, though
not the same eyes; yet so little do they betray any external
appearance of injury, that they are as unclouded and bright
as the eyes of those who most distinctly see. In this instance
alone I am a dissembler against my will. My face, which
is said to indicate a total privation of blood, is of a complexion entirely opposite to the pale and the cadaverous;
so that, though I am more than forty years old, there is
scarcely any one to whom I do not appear ten years
younger than I am; and the smoothness of my skin is
not in the least affected by the wrinkles of age. If there
be one particle of falsehood in this relation, I should

deservedly incur the ridicule of many thousands of my countrymen, and even many foreigners to whom I am personally known. But if he, in a matter so foreign to his purpose, shall be found to have asserted so many shameless and gratuitous falsehoods, you may the more readily estimate the quantity of his veracity on other topics. Thus much necessity compelled me to assert concerning my personal appearance. Respecting yours, though I have been informed that it is most insignificant and contemptible, a perfect mirror of the worthlessness of your character and the malevolence of your heart, I say nothing, and no one will be anxious that anything should be said. I wish that I could with equal facility refute what this barbarous opponent has said of my blindness; but I cannot do it, and I must submit to the affliction. It is not so wretched to be blind as it is not to be capable of enduring blindness. But why should I not endure a misfortune which it behooves every one to be prepared to endure if it should happen; which may, in the common course of things, happen to any man; and which has been known to happen to the most distinguished and virtuous persons in history.

And in short, did not our Saviour himself clearly declare that the poor man whom He restored to sight had not been born blind either on account of his own sins or those of his progenitors? And with respect to myself, though I have accurately examined my conduct and scrutinized my soul, I call thee, O God, the searcher of hearts, to witness that I am not conscious, either in the more early or in the later periods of my life, of having committed any enormity which might deservedly have marked me out as a fit object for such a calamitous visitation. But since my enemies boast that this affliction is only a retribution for the transgressions of my pen, I again invoke the Almighty to witness that I never, at any time, wrote anything which I did not think agreeable to truth, to justice, and to piety. This was my persuasion then, and I feel the same persuasion now. Nor was I ever prompted to such exertions by the influence of ambition, by the lust of lucre or of praise; it was only by the conviction of duty and the feeling of patriotism, a disinterested passion for the extension of civil and religious liberty. Thus, therefore, when I was publicly solicited to write a reply to the Defense of the royal cause, when I had to contend with the pressure of sickness and with the apprehension of soon losing the sight of my remaining eye, and when my medical attendants clearly announced that if I did engage in the work, it would be irreparably lost, their premonitions caused no hesitation and inspired no dismay. I would not have listened to the voice even of Esculapius himself from the shrine of Epidaurus, in preference to the suggestions of the heavenly monitor within my breast; my resolution was unshaken, though the alternative was either the loss of my sight or the desertion of my duty: and I called to mind those two destinies which the oracle of Delphi announced to the son of Thetis:

> Two fates may lead me to the realms of night;
> If staying here, around Troy's wall I fight,
> To my dear home no more must I return;
> But lasting glory will adorn my urn.
> But, if I withdraw from the martial strife,
> Short is my fame, but long will be my life.
> *Iliad* ix, 410–15

I considered that many had purchased a less good by a greater evil, the meed of glory by the loss of life; but that I might procure great good by little suffering; that though I am blind, I might still discharge the most honorable duties, the performance of which, as it is something more durable than glory, ought to be an object of superior admiration and esteem; I resolved, therefore, to make the short interval of sight which was left me to enjoy as beneficial as possible to the public interest. Thus it is clear by what motives I was governed in the measures which I took, and the losses which I sustained. Let then the calumniators of the divine goodness cease to revile, or to make me the object of their superstitious imaginations. Let them consider that my situation, such as it is, is neither an object of my shame or my regret, that my resolutions are too firm to be

shaken, that I am not depressed by any sense of the divine
displeasure; that, on the other hand, in the most momentous
periods, I have had full experience of the divine favor and
protection; and that, in the solace and the strength which
have been infused into me from above, I have been enabled
to do the will of God; that I may oftener think on what He
has bestowed than on what He has withheld; that, in short,
I am unwilling to exchange my consciousness of rectitude
with that of any other person; and that I feel the recollection a treasured store of tranquillity and delight.

I will now mention who and whence I am. I was born in
London of an honest family; my father was distinguished by
the undeviating integrity of his life; my mother, by the
esteem in which she was held and the alms which she bestowed. My father destined me from a child to the pursuits
of literature; and my appetite for knowledge was so vora-
cious that, from twelve years of age, I hardly ever left my
studies or went to bed before midnight. This primarily led
to my loss of sight. My eyes were naturally weak, and I was
subject to frequent headaches; which, however, could not
chill the ardor of my curiosity or retard the progress of my
improvement. My father had me daily instructed in the
grammar-school and by other masters at home. He then,
after I had acquired a proficiency in various languages and
had made a considerable progress in philosophy, sent me
to the University of Cambridge. Here I passed seven years
in the usual course of instruction and study, with the approbation of the good and without any stain upon my character, till I took the degree of Master of Arts. After this I did
not, as this miscreant feigns, run away into Italy, but of my
own accord retired to my father's house, whither I was accompanied by the regrets of most of the Fellows of the College, who showed me no common marks of friendship and
esteem. On my father's estate, where he had determined to
pass the remainder of his days, I enjoyed an interval of
uninterrupted leisure which I entirely devoted to the perusal of the Greek and Latin classics; though I occasionally
visited the metropolis, either for the sake of purchasing

books or of learning something new in mathematics or in music, in which I, at that time, found a source of pleasure and amusement.

In this manner I spent five years till my mother's death. I then became anxious to visit foreign parts and particularly Italy. My father gave me his permission, and I left home with one servant. On my departure the celebrated Henry Wotton,[4] who had long been King James's ambassador at Venice, gave me a signal proof of his regard, in an elegant letter which he wrote, breathing not only the warmest friendship but containing some maxims of conduct which I found very useful in my travels. The noble Thomas Scudamore,[5] King Charles's ambassador, to whom I carried letters of recommendation, received me most courteously at Paris. His lordship gave me a card of introduction to the learned Hugo Grotius,[6] at that time ambassador from the Queen of Sweden to the French court, whose acquaintance I anxiously desired and to whose house I was accompanied by some of his lordship's friends. A few days after, when I set out for Italy, he gave me letters to the English merchants on my route, that they might show me any civilities in their power.

Taking ship at Nice, I arrived at Genoa, and afterwards visited Leghorn, Pisa, and Florence. In the latter city, which I have always more particularly esteemed for the elegance of its dialect, its genius, and its taste, I stopped about two months, when I contracted an intimacy with many persons of rank and learning and was a constant attendant at their literary parties, a practice which prevails there and tends so much to the diffusion of knowledge and the preservation of friendship. No time will ever abolish the agreeable recollections which I cherish of Jacopo Gaddi, Carlo Dati,

[4] Wotton diplomat and friend of John Donne; author of the famous definition, "an ambassador is one who lies abroad for the good of his country."   [5] Scudamore in fact John Scudamore, a friend of Grotius   [6] Grotius author of "The Law of War and Peace," the first great book on international law

Frescobaldi, Caltellini, Bonmattei, Clementillo, Francini,[7] and many others. From Florence I went to Siena, thence to Rome, where, after I had spent about two months in viewing the antiquities of that renowned city, where I experienced the most friendly attentions from Lucas Holsten[8] and other learned and ingenious men, I continued my route to Naples. There I was introduced by a certain recluse, with whom I had travelled from Rome, to John Baptista Manso,[9] Marquis of Villa, a nobleman of distinguished rank and authority, to whom Torquato Tasso, the illustrious poet, inscribed his book on friendship. During my stay he gave me singular proofs of his regard: he himself conducted me round the city and to the palace of the viceroy, and more than once paid me a visit at my lodgings. On my departure he gravely apologized for not having shown me more civility, which he said he had been restrained from doing because I had spoken with so little reserve on matters of religion.

When I was preparing to pass over into Sicily and Greece, the melancholy intelligence which I received of the civil commotions in England made me alter my purpose, for I thought it base to be travelling for amusement abroad while my fellow-citizens were fighting for liberty at home. While I was on my way back to Rome, some merchants informed me that the English Jesuits had formed a plot against me if I returned to Rome because I had spoken too freely on religion; for it was a rule which I laid down to myself in those places never to be the first to begin any conversation on religion, but if any questions were put to me concerning my faith, to declare it without any reserve or fear. I, nevertheless, returned to Rome. I took no steps to conceal either my person or my character; and for about the space of two months I again openly defended, as I had done before, the reformed religion in the very metropolis

[7] Gaddi . . . Francini literary men whom Milton met in Florence, most of them members of the literary society mentioned p. 77  [8] Holsten librarian at the Vatican  [9] Manso a patron and friend of the poet in Tasso's later years and his biographer

of popery. By the favor of God I got safe back to Florence, where I was received with as much affection as if I had returned to my native country. There I stopped as many months as I had done before, except that I made an excursion for a few days to Lucca, and crossing the Apennines, passed through Bologna and Ferrara to Venice.

After I had spent a month in surveying the curiosities of this city, and had put on board a ship the books which I had collected in Italy, I proceeded through Verona and Milan, and along the Leman Lake to Geneva. The mention of this city brings to my recollection the slandering More, and makes me again call the Deity to witness that in all those places in which vice meets with so little discouragement, and is practiced with so little shame, I never once deviated from the paths of integrity and virtue, and perpetually reflected that, though my conduct might escape the notice of men, it could not elude the inspection of God. At Geneva I held daily conferences with John Deodati,[10] the learned professor of theology. Then pursuing my former route through France, I returned to my native country after an absence of one year and about three months, at the time when Charles, having broken the peace, was renewing what is called the "Bishops' War" with the Scots, in which the royalists being routed in the first encounter,[11] and the English being universally and justly disaffected, the necessity of his affairs at last obliged him to convene a parliament.[12] As soon as I was able, I hired a spacious house in the city for myself and my books, where I again with rapture renewed my literary pursuits and where I calmly awaited the issue of the contest, which I trusted to the wise conduct of Providence and to the courage of the people.

The vigor of the parliament had begun to humble the pride of the bishops. As long as the liberty of speech was no longer subject to control, all mouths began to be opened

[10] Deodati translator of the Bible into Italian; uncle of Milton's Cambridge friend, Charles Diodati    [11] Encounter, August, 1639    [12] parliament the Short Parliament called in April, 1640, followed by the Long Parliament called in November

against the bishops; some complained of the vices of the individuals, others of those of the order. They said that it was unjust that they alone should differ from the model of other reformed churches;[13] that the government of the church should be according to the pattern of other churches, and particularly the word of God. This awakened all my attention and my zeal. I saw that a way was opening for the establishment of real liberty; that the foundation was laying for the deliverance of man from the yoke of slavery and superstition; that the principles of religion, which were the first objects of our care, would exert a salutary influence on the manners and constitution of the republic; and as I had from my youth studied the distinctions between religious and civil rights, I perceived that if I ever wished to be of use, I ought at least not to be wanting to my country, to the church, and to so many of my fellow-Christians, in a crisis of so much danger; I therefore determined to relinquish the other pursuits in which I was engaged and to transfer the whole force of my talents and my industry to this one important object. I accordingly wrote two books[14] to a friend concerning the reformation of the church of England. Afterwards, when two bishops[15] of superior distinction vindicated their privileges against some principal ministers, I thought that on those topics, to the consideration of which I was led solely by my love of truth and my reverence for Christianity, I should not probably write worse than those who were contending only for their own emoluments and usurpations. I therefore answered the one in two books, of which the first is inscribed *Of Prelatical Episcopacy*, and the other *The Reason of Church-Government*; and I replied to the other in some *Animadversions*, and soon after in an *Apology*. On this occasion it was supposed that I brought a timely succor to the ministery, who

[13] differ . . . churches in retaining bishops rather than going to a presbyterian system  [14] two books *Of Reformation in England* (in two books), 1641  [15] two bishops James Usher (or Ussher), Archbishop of Armagh, and Joseph Hall, Bishop of Exeter and later of Norwich

were hardly a match for the eloquence of their opponents; and from that time I was actively employed in refuting any answers that appeared.

When the bishops could no longer resist the multitude of their assailants, I had leisure to turn my thoughts to other subjects; to the promotion of real and substantial liberty, which is rather to be sought from within than from without, and whose existence depends not so much on the terror of the sword as on sobriety of conduct and integrity of life. When, therefore, I perceived that there were three species of liberty which are essential to the happiness of social life—religious, domestic, and civil; and as I had already written concerning the first, and the magistrates were strenuously active in obtaining the third, I determined to turn my attention to the second or the domestic species. As this seemed to involve three material questions, the conditions of the conjugal tie, the education of the children, and the free publication of the thoughts, I made them objects of distinct consideration. I explained my sentiments not only concerning the solemnization of marriage but the dissolution, if circumstances rendered it necessary; and I drew my arguments from the divine law, which Christ did not abolish or publish another more grievous than that of Moses. I stated my own opinions, and those of others, concerning the exclusive exception of fornication, which our illustrious Selden has since,[16] in his "Hebrew Wife," more copiously discussed; for he in vain makes a vaunt of liberty in the senate or in the forum who languishes under the vilest servitude to an inferior at home. On this subject, therefore, I published some books which were more particularly necessary at that time, when man and wife were often the most inveterate foes, when the man often staid to take care of his children at home, while the mother of the family was seen in the camp of the enemy threatening death and destruction to her husband. I then discussed the principles of education in a summary manner, but suffi-

---

[16] Selden . . . since in 1646

ciently copious for those who attend seriously to the subject; than which nothing can be more necessary to principle the minds of men in virtue, the only genuine source of political and individual liberty, the only true safeguard of states, the bulwark of their prosperity and renown. Lastly, I wrote my *Areopagitica*, in order to deliver the press from the restraints with which it was encumbered, that the power of determining what was true and what was false, what ought to be published and what to be suppressed, might no longer be entrusted to a few illiterate and illiberal individuals, who refused their sanction to any work which contained views or sentiments at all above the level of the vulgar superstition.

On the last species of civil liberty I said nothing, because I saw that sufficient attention was paid to it by the magistrates; nor did I write anything on the prerogative of the crown, till the King, voted an enemy by the parliament and vanquished in the field, was summoned before the tribunal which condemned him to lose his head. But when, at length, some Presbyterian ministers, who had formerly been the most bitter enemies to Charles, became jealous of the growth of the Independents and of their ascendancy in the parliament, most tumultuously clamored against the sentence, and did all in their power to prevent the execution, though they were not angry so much on account of the act itself as because it was not the act of their party; and when they dared to affirm that the doctrine of the Protestants, and of all the reformed churches, was abhorrent to such an atrocious proceeding against kings, I thought that it became me to oppose such a glaring falsehood; and accordingly, without any immediate or personal application to Charles, I showed, in an abstract consideration of the question, what might lawfully be done against tyrants;[17] and in support of what I advanced produced the opinions of the most celebrated divines, while I vehemently in-

---

[17] showed . . . tyrants *The Tenure of Kings and Magistrates,* 1649

veighed against the egregious ignorance or effrontery of
men who professed better things, and from whom better
things might have been expected. That book did not make
its appearance till after the death of Charles; and was
written rather to reconcile the minds of the people to the
event than to discuss the legitimacy of that particular sentence, which concerned the magistrates and which was
already executed.

Such were the fruits of my private studies, which I
gratuitously presented to the church and to the state, and
for which I was recompensed by nothing but impunity;
though the actions themselves procured me peace of conscience and the approbation of the good, while I exercised
that freedom of discussion which I loved. Others, without
labor or desert, got possession of honors and emoluments;
but no one ever knew me either soliciting anything myself
or through the medium of my friends, ever beheld me in
a supplicating posture at the doors of the senate or the
levees of the great. I usually kept myself secluded at home,
where my own property, part of which had been withheld
during the civil commotions and part of which had been
absorbed in the oppressive contributions which I had to
sustain, afforded me a scanty subsistence. When I was released from these engagements and thought that I was
about to enjoy an interval of uninterrupted ease, I turned
my thoughts to a continued history of my country from the
earliest times to the present period. I had already finished
four books, when, after the subversion of the monarchy and
the establishment of a republic, I was surprised by an in-
vitation from the Council of State, who desired my services
in the office for foreign affairs. A book appeared soon after
which was ascribed to the king and contained the most
invidious charges against the parliament. I was ordered to
answer it; and opposed the Iconoclast[18] to his Icon. I did

[18] Iconoclast *Eikonklastes*, 1649 (The Image Breaker), written
in answer to *Eikon Basilike, The True Portraiture of His Sacred
Majesty in His Solitude and Sufferings*, 1649, which purported
to have been written by Charles I

not insult over fallen majesty, as is pretended; I only preferred Queen Truth to King Charles. The charge of insult, which I saw that the malevolent would urge, I was at some pains to remove in the beginning of the work, and as often as possible in other places. Salmasius then appeared, to whom they were not, as More says, long in looking about for an opponent, but immediately appointed me, who happened at the time to be present in the Council. I have thus, sir, given some account of myself, in order to stop your mouth and to remove any prejudices which your falsehoods and misrepresentations might cause even good men to entertain against me.

# BIBLIOGRAPHY

### EDITIONS

*Works,* 20 vols., edited by F. A. Patterson and others. New York, 1931-1940.

*The Student's Milton,* rev. ed., edited by F. A. Patterson. New York, 1933.

*Areopagitica,* 3rd ed., edited with Introduction and Notes by John W. Hales. Oxford, 1882.

*Areopagitica,* with a Commentary by Sir Richard C. Jebb and with Supplemental Material. Cambridge, 1918.

*Milton on Education,* edited with an Introduction and Notes by Oliver Morley Ainsworth. New Haven, 1928.

### INTERPRETATIONS

Barker, Arthur E., *Milton and the Puritan Dilemma.* Toronto, 1942.

Bush, Douglas, *John Milton: A Sketch of His Life and Writings.* New York, 1964.

Gooch, G. P., *English Democratic Ideas in the Seventeenth Century,* 2nd ed. Cambridge, 1927.

———, *Political Thought in England from Bacon to Halifax.* Home University Library, London, 1914.

Grierson, Herbert, *Milton and Wordsworth.* New York, 1937.

Haller, William, *Liberty and Reformation in the Puritan Revolution.* New York, 1955.

Haller, William, *Tracts on Liberty in the Puritan Revolution, 1638-1647,* 3 vols., edited with a commentary. Vol. I, Commentary. New York, 1934.

———, *The Rise of Puritanism.* New York, 1938.

Hanford, James Holly, *A Milton Handbook,* 4th ed. New York, 1946.

———, *John Milton, Englishman.* New York, 1949.

Tillyard, E. M. W., *Milton.* New York, 1930; 1947.

———, *The Miltonic Setting.* Cambridge, 1938.

109

Wolfe, Don M., *Milton in the Puritan Revolution.* New York, 1941.

Woodhouse, A. S. P., *Puritanism and Liberty.* London, 1938; Chicago, 1951.